Published by **National Historic Ships** in 2010

Park Row, Greenwich, London, SE10 9NF
www.nationalhistoricships.org.uk

© **National Historic Ships** 2010

All rights reserved
ISBN 978-0-9566554-0-0

Supported by

Design & layout by

Christian Topf Design Ltd
www.ctd-studio.co.uk

Printed by Park Lane Press, UK

Printed on FSC certified paper, using vegetable based inks, power from 100% renewable resources and waterless printing technology. Print production systems registered to ISO 14001: 2004, ISO 9001: 2008 and EMAS standards

Disclaimer: The authors and publishers accept no liability for personal injury, property damage or loss as a result of actions inspired by this book. The information given here is for guidance only and represents the best advice on good practice as at the date of publication. Conservation can be contentious and it is for owners to make the judgements appropriate for their vessel, or seek specific advice in relation to their circumstances. Conservation work can also be dangerous and due care should always be taken. National Historic Ships has made every effort to ensure that the information given in this book is accurate and accepts no liability for any errors, omissions or misleading statements.

CONSERVING
HISTORIC VESSELS

UNDERSTANDING HISTORIC VESSELS | **VOLUME 3**

This book was commissioned by members of the

Advisory Committee on National Historic Ships:

Dr. Robert Prescott, Chairman; John Kearon; Captain David Newberry RN;
Dr. Campbell McMurray OBE; Roger Hanbury; Matthew Tanner MBE;
Jane Ryder; Sean Neeson (co-opted); Mike Lewis; John Robinson;
Captain Simon Waite; Tim Parr; David Jenkins (co-opted).

ACKNOWLEDGMENTS

We would like to thank the following institutions and individuals for their help and assistance in the production of this book:

FUNDING SUPPORT:
Society for Nautical Research (SNR);
The Headley Trust.

IMAGE CREDITS:
Alfred Corry Trust (184); Andy Wyke, National Maritime Museum Cornwall (145); A R Trenear (166); Australian National Maritime Museum (171); Cambria Trust (148); Chris Jones (174); Christian Topf (collage, opposite forward, 29, 37, 50, 69, 89, 92-93); City College Plymouth (6); Commanding Officer, HMS *Victory* (75); Davey & Company London Ltd (2-3, 12, 14 far left & left, 15 far left & right top & bottom, 16, 17 middle bottom right & far right, 32-33, 41, 42-43, 51, 65, 70-71, 81, 96-97, 103, 104, 123, 133, 147, 150-151, 159, 179, 189); Dundee Heritage Trust (79); family of James and Marguerite McBey (63, 64); Gemma Stunt, Boat Building Academy Ltd (176); Guy Standen (contents); James Dodds & the Jardine Press (front cover, 17 top, 17 middle right & left, 17 bottom left, 110-111, 127, 136-137, 162-163); Jo Cox (7 left, 19 left, 20 right, 26, 30-31, 57, 86-87, 90, 100, 138-139, 173); John Kearon; John Robinson; Kampfner Photography (39, 106-107); Lakeland Arts Trust (134); Lord Ambrose Greenway (34-35); Luke Powell, Working Sail (38, 164-165, 167); Medusa Trust (10-11); Merseyside Maritime Museum/National Museums Liverpool (19 middle, 20 left, 40, 44-45, 61, 128-129, 131, 143); Michael Bull (118); National Maritime Museum Greenwich London (standfirst, 9, 15 near left, 21 right, 22, 25 left & middle, 54-55, 62, 66, 67, 68, 77 top, 80, 84-85, 101, 132, 183, 187, 194, 196, 202, endpaper); National Museum of Ireland (4-5, 21 left, 112-113, 117, 124); National Waterways Museum (47); Owners of Vessels on the National Register of Historic Vessels – *Doris* (20 middle), *Edith May* (46), *George Elmy* (102), *Helen II* (48-49), *Mikado* (7 right), *President* (19 right), *Saturn* (7 middle); Pauline Rook Photography; Ray Sutcliffe (169); Ron Ellis (98-99); Royal National Lifeboat Institution (18, 158, 160); Shipshape & Bristol Fashion (175); South Eastern Tug Society; ss Great Britain Trust (72-73, 114, 122, 157); St. Fagans, National History Museum (25 right); Stirling & Son (144); Swedish National Maritime Museums, Annelie Karlsson (121); Thames Steamers (180-181); The Scottish Fisheries Museum (156, 185); Tim Kirton (140); Tom Cunliffe (77 bottom, 190, 191, 192, 193); Trinity Sailing (21, middle); Unicorn Preservation Society (59); Windermere Steamboat Museum; WPT/Roy Riley (8).

CONSULTEES:
Adrian Birtles, Steam Boat Association; Adrian Osler; Alan Aberg; Alan Watson, HMS *Medusa*; Alison Richardson, CEO Institute of Conservation; Andrew Gladwell, Paddle Steamer Preservation Society (PSPS); Andrew Rowley,

The National Archives (TNA); Andy King, Bristol Museum & Art Gallery; Andy Wyke, National Maritime Museum Cornwall (NMMC); Ann Coats, SNR; Bill Puddle, Maritime Workshop; Brad King, HMS *Belfast*; Brian Patterson, SNR; Brian Smith; Captain R M Woodman; Carole Souter, Heritage Lottery Fund (HLF); Charles Betts; Charles Payton; Colin Allen; Dame Fiona Reynolds, National Trust; D Hobbs, SNR; David Clement; David Daines, Historic Narrow Boat Owners Club; David Dickinson, Imperial College; David Morgan, Heritage Afloat (HA); David Ralph, Maritime & Coastguard Agency (MCA); David Watkinson, Cardiff University; Des Pawson MBE, Footrope Knots; Diane Lees, Imperial War Museum; Dominic Tweddle, National Museum of the Royal Navy; Douglas McElvogue; Dr Dan Atkinson, Headland Archaeology; Dr David Chalmers; Dr Mark Jones, *Mary Rose*; Dr Roger Knight; Edmund Lee, English Heritage (EH); Eric Kentley; Frank Moris, Sailing Barges Association; Fred Aldsworth; George Hogg, National Small Boat Register (NSBR); George Monger; Hester Marriott, Headley Trust; Ian Clark; Ian McMillian, Waverley Excursions Ltd; Ian Whitehead, Tyne and Wear Museums; Jerry Lewis, Dunkirk Little Ships Restoration Trust; Jim Tildesley, Scottish Maritime Museum; Jo Cox, Keystone Historic Buildings; Jo Lawler, Maritime Curators Group; John Bethell, SNR; John Bingeman, SNR; John Paton; John Peach; Jonathan Carr; Jonathan Griffin, NMMC; Jonathan Seagrave, South West Maritime History Society; Kate Pugh, Heritage Alliance; Katherine Doyle, PRISM Fund; Keith Chittenden, SNR; Kevin Fewster, National Maritime Museum (NMM); Kew Bridge Steam Museum; Laura Rigby, Department of Culture, Media & Sport (DCMS); Larry Robbins; Len Patterson; Malcolm Brown; Mark Dunkley, EH; Mark Horton; Michael Dalton, SNR; Michael Williams, SNR; Mike Stammers; Mike Turpin; Nancy Ritchie-Noakes; Nicholas Coney, TNA; Nick Walker; Nicola Alford, *Bessie Ellen*; Nigel Rigby, International Congress of Maritime Museums; Norman Cary, Historic Naval Ships Association (USA); Paul Evans, New Zealand Maritime Museum; Paul Merrington, Gweek Quay Ltd; Paul Ridgway, World Ship Trust; Peter Collins, Waterways Trust; Peter Dodds; Peter Hollins, Maritime Workshop; Peter Hore, SNR; Peter Nash, SNR; Peter Williams, Bodinnick Boatyard; Prof. Sarah Palmer, Greenwich Maritime Institute; Rachel Mulhearn, Merseyside Maritime Museum; Ranald McGuiness, Historic Scotland; Ray Sutcliffe, HA; Reg Harris, SNR; Richard Bateman, SNR; Richard Harding, SNR; Richard Holdsworth, The Historic Dockyard, Chatham; Robert Holden, Old Gaffers Association; Robert Mowat, Royal Commission on the Ancient & Historical Monuments of Scotland; Robert Preston, SNR; Rod Ward-Horner, TNA; Roger Fuller; Roy Clare CBE, Museums, Libraries & Archives; Simon Stephens, NMM; Sir Julian Oswald; Sir Neil Cossons OBE; Sir Robert Crawford; Stephen Riley; Thedo Fruithof, European Maritime Heritage; Tom Cunliffe; Tommy Nielsen, T Nielson & Company Ltd; Tom Peppitt, SNR; Trefor Thorpe, Welsh Assembly, CADW; Trevor Blakely, Royal Institute of Naval Architects; Will Stirling, Stirling & Son; Wyn Davies, Frazer Nash.

FOREWORD

The United Kingdom is richly endowed with historic ships and boats, over 1,000 of which are listed on the National Register of Historic Vessels (NRHV) including some 200 of pre-eminent significance which make up the National Historic Fleet. These vessels comprise a broad spectrum of functions and types such as warships, merchantmen, fishing, leisure, service and passenger vessels. The Register embraces inland, coastal and deep-sea craft and, together with those on the National Small Boat Register (NSBR) which is administered by the National Maritime Museum Cornwall, provides a magnificent overview of our surviving maritime heritage.

I have been maintaining, operating and researching historic vessels for over thirty years and have long been aware of the difficulties faced by those seeking to conserve this remarkable yet vulnerable aspect of our heritage. Ships are built of highly perishable materials in comparison with built forms on land, and in most cases the result is a relatively short life-expectancy. Until the establishment of the Advisory Committee on National Historic Ships in 2006, there was no over-arching UK body responsible for promoting the interests of historic vessels and no single source of advice addressing the problems of conservation.

National Historic Ships, funded by the Department for Culture Media and Sport, is heir to the work of the independent National Historic Ships Committee, which pioneered the creation of the NRHV based upon a quantitative assessment of heritage merit in ships. National Historic Ships now manages the Register and is the chief source of expertise, advising government and other bodies on all matters relating to historic vessels. We also administer a small grants scheme for the owners and operators of these craft: a major innovation and the first example of direct government financial assistance to historic ships.

Conserving Historic Vessels sets out to guide vessel custodians (irrespective of whether or not their vessels are on the NRHV) through the complexities of conserving historic ships for future generations. This volume is the third in the series, *Understanding Historic Vessels*, with the two earlier volumes published online, covering the recording of historic vessels and, in cases where all other options have been explored, their controlled deconstruction. Together, the three volumes form an invaluable compendium of guidance on methods for conserving our maritime past.

It is important to explain that this volume does not set out to cover the minutiae of ship-building and repair techniques, but instead defines the principles underpinning conservation. It guides readers through the options and difficult choices they face

FOREWORD

when formulating the best conservation approach. Each historic ship presents a unique set of problems and so the conservation strategy must be tailored to the individual vessel. This publication is supported by an online bibliography and technical papers which will be updated as conservation science extends knowledge. The book also devotes a chapter to the growing number of replica vessels, which deserve our attention both to ensure a clearer rationalisation for their building and to help funding bodies assess the value of these projects.

This volume has drawn upon the knowledge and expertise of many people. The project was led by two highly experienced and respected individuals: Jo Cox contributed a deep understanding of conservation and management issues, whilst Matthew Tanner brought a breadth of knowledge and a keen critical awareness of the best science-based conservation techniques which proved invaluable. Martyn Heighton and Hannah Cunliffe developed and refined the content, drawing upon the extremely constructive contributions sent to us by the wide range of maritime and conservation experts with whom we consulted. Hannah also worked closely with Christian Topf to create the striking design which is a mark of this publication. From its origin to its conclusion this has been a collegiate exercise.

Finally, it is my pleasure to record the Committee's gratitude for the support we have received. Many of the images and illustrations were generously provided free of charge, with a large number supplied by the Chairman and Trustees of the National Maritime Museum and the cover image, as well as some internal prints by artist James Dodds. The Headley Trust grant-aided the project as part of an award to promote skills training and the Society for Nautical Research (SNR) helped cover the final production costs. The latter's support is particularly apposite given the SNR's pre-eminence in ship conservation, having established the 'Save the Victory Fund' in 1922, and the fact that this book has been published in 2010, the centenary year of the Society's birth.

R G W Prescott
Chairman, National Historic Ships

CONTENTS

2	INTRODUCTION
12	**HOW TO USE THIS BOOK**
18	CONSERVATION PRINCIPLES
22	HISTORY OF CONSERVATION
28	CONSERVATION FUNDING IN THE UK & ABROAD
32	1. EARLY VESSEL EVALUATION & ACQUISITION
42	2. STABILISATION
52	3. UNDERSTANDING
70	4. ASSESSING SIGNIFICANCE
84	**5. THE CONSERVATION GATEWAY**
96	6. IDENTIFYING RISKS TO SIGNIFICANCE & EVALUATING VIABILITY
104	7. BEYOND THE GATEWAY: CONSERVATION PROCESSES
110	7.1 PRESERVATION — FABRIC ROUTE
126	7.2 RESTORATION —
136	**7.3 RECONSTRUCTION** — OPERATIONAL ROUTE
150	**7.4 ADAPTATION** —
162	8. REPLICATION
178	9. MAINTENANCE
196	DEFINITIONS
202	BIBLIOGRAPHY
208	INDEX

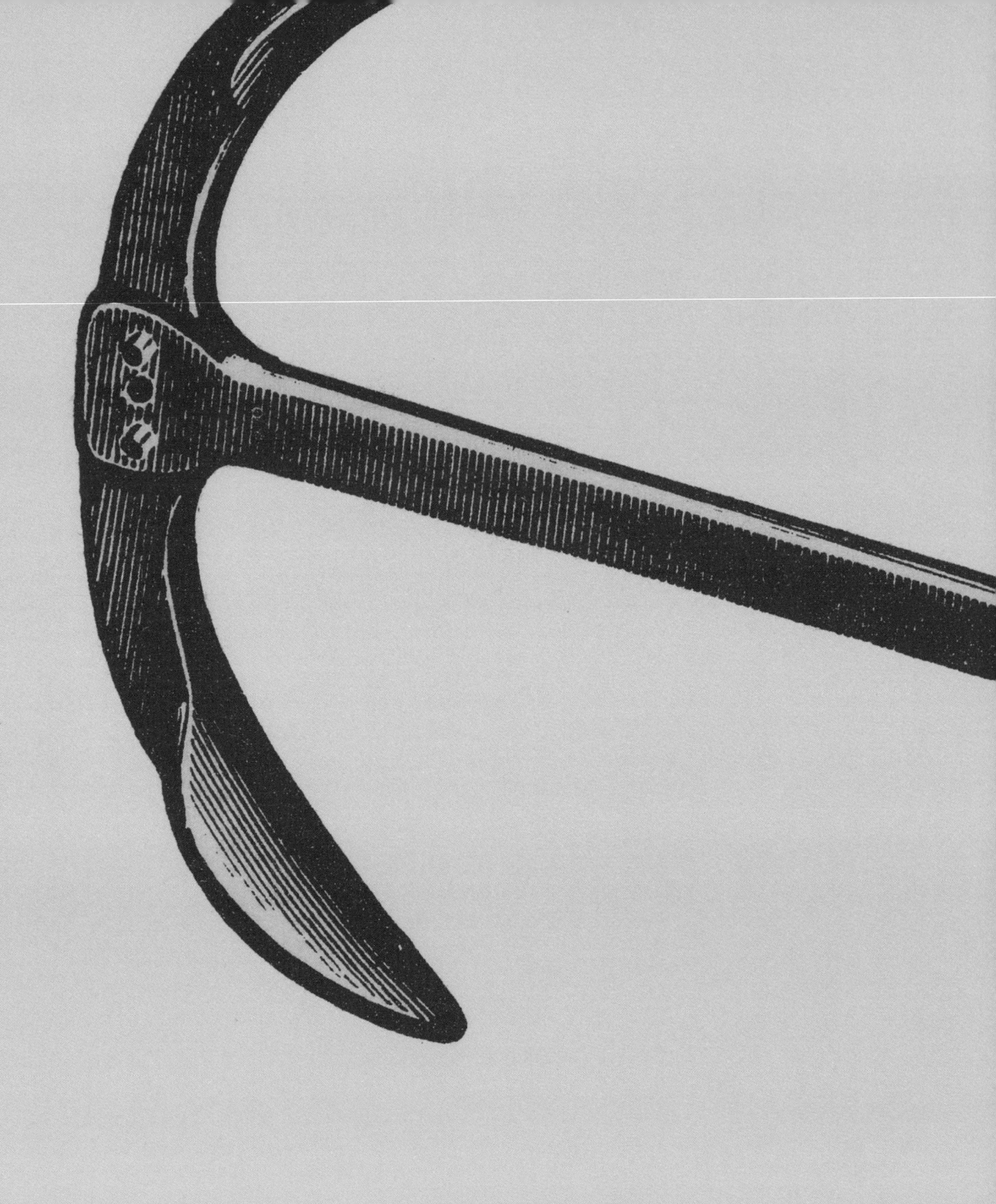

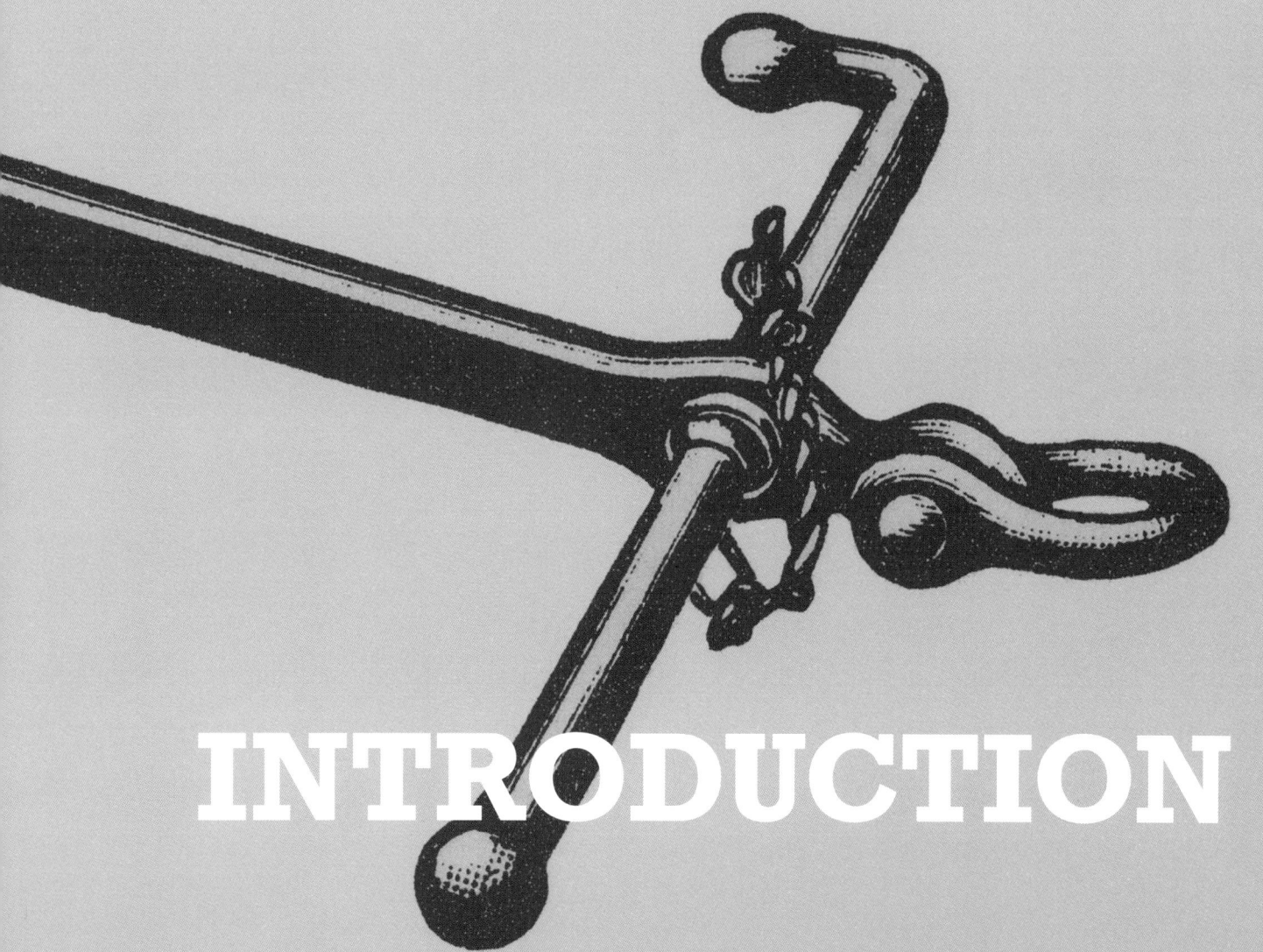

INTRODUCTION

what is this book all about?

INTRODUCTION

Ships and boats are some of the most complex human artefacts designed at any time in history. Diverse in scale and type, they have immense emotional impact as expressions, functional and often beautiful, of people's ingenuity in relation to their environment. They have generated cultural change on a grand scale, affecting people who never set foot on a vessel.

A student at City College Plymouth learns how to work with wood. Specialist techniques and a good understanding of materials are integral to both the creation and survival of UK vessels.

They are not an isolated category of creations, but are intertwined with places, objects and archives. They were, and are, part of people's lives and human interaction: local, national and international. All boats and ships reflect the history of people as skilled craftsmen, inventors, and risk takers. Great warships and ocean going trading vessels remind us of the history of international politics, economies and national prestige. Working boats, with their striking or subtle regional variations, are the foundation of many local settlements that took root and developed where boats could be launched and landed. The importance of ships and boats to the culture and history of the UK should not be underestimated.

The human element looking after historic vessels today is as varied in form and character as their boats and ships. Private individuals own and care for a large proportion of the UK's historic vessels. A single owner may stubbornly work against the financial odds to return a small wooden boat to a condition where she can be sailed for personal pleasure. Groups of enthusiasts collaborate to research, use and often rescue a particular type of vessel. Small businesses and trusts keep historic vessels in commercial use, chartering or using them for sail training. Some boats and ships are public or charitable assets, either as a single object amongst others in a local museum, or part of larger, professionally curated maritime collections or stand alone trusts, often supported by teams of volunteers, and displayed and interpreted to the public. The input of trained volunteers is invaluable both for static and operational vessels. However, experience has shown that operational vessels are particularly attractive to potential volunteers as they give opportunities to maintain and use working equipment and, in many instances, the chance to play an active part in rallies, festivals and events.

This book has been designed by National Historic Ships to identify principles and guidelines for the conservation of historic vessels (whether built for use at sea or in fresh water) in the 21st Century, as well as offering practical advice and signposting standards of best practice. The aim of conserving historic vessels is to retain their significance or what it is that matters about them and to pass it on to future generations. This book does not offer definitive guidelines on the practicalities of conservation because every vessel is different. However, it does set out the values behind the various conservation processes, encouraging owners to think about ethics in relation to the work they are doing. It is intended to provide a toolkit of sound principles that are equally of use to private owners, groups of enthusiasts, trusts and museums.

There has always been discussion in maritime circles about how best or to what extent any particular vessel should be repaired, restored, or preserved. This has led to fragmentations of views, and widely differing approaches, standards, and outcomes. Other parts of the heritage world have had to address similar difficulties and challenges – how to preserve historic vehicles, stately homes, or historic aircraft for example. Accordingly, there is much hard-won experience that can help everyone to find a thoughtful and satisfactory way forward for their own particular challenges. This book draws on that knowledge to bring together a logical formula which can be used in any heritage project to achieve the best possible outcome.

Above: Historic ships are conserved in many different ways for different purposes – as static exhibits, for pleasure in private ownership or for commercial use. This diversity is reflected in the conservation route that is adopted in each particular case.

Previous double page spread: Preservation work nearing completion on the frames and hull planking of Erskine Childers' yacht, Asgard.

It is important to define what is meant by conservation. For some, simply making a vessel fit for sea could be construed as conservation, regardless of the changes that her fabric has undergone in the process. However, this is not necessarily conservation as defined by National Historic Ships, because the work has not been designed to record or maintain her significance and pass it on to future generations. Conservation at the highest standard is not for everybody, nor should it be expected for all old boats and ships. Simply keeping a vessel operational is a huge challenge. Conservation should be determined by the significance of the vessel; it demands that a well-judged sense of all her historic values and meanings is placed at the forefront, and subsequently at the heart, of any work carried out. If compromises have to be made and one value can only be conserved at the expense of another, the reasons for this should be based on sound conservation principles. Equally, any subsequent method of repair, restoration or reconstruction must then be compatible with an agreed sense of her historic value.

The survival of original fabric, a key concept in conservation, is in conflict with an essential part of the design of historic vessels, that is, the requirement to move and be used on the water with the aid of human skills. Operational use brings obvious risks, including potential loss and subjects the vessel to a harsh environment. Water, fresh or salt, impacts on wood, metal and other materials in complex ways. Wood is vulnerable to insect damage in addition to wet and dry rot. Ferrous metal corrodes and iron or steel fastenings in wooden boats, in the presence of seawater, can generate uniquely difficult conservation problems. A ship's fabric will always need regular minor work, then more major maintenance, and thus the historic material of the vessel is gradually eroded, repair on repair, and replaced by modern fabric.

On the other hand, operating an historic vessel maintains human skills of seamanship, boat repair, and a connection to the working environment of an historic vessel. However, the strength of that connection depends on how authentic her use is. Few historic vessels can claim an unbroken continuity of original use and repair by an original owner or craftsman. Most have come to the end of their working lives, and ceased to operate or be maintained as they once were, long before they come into heritage use. Many historic-looking vessels, marketed and bought on the grounds that they seem old, or 'historic', may have scarcely any original fabric left and be no more than a contemporary view of what the vessel might, or could have been, rather than what she actually was.

Similarly, a static vessel has also lost a key part of her design purpose. Like vessels in operational use, static vessels kept in the open are vulnerable to all the damage that weathering can bring. Yet static conservation can also allow more fabric to be kept,

Facing page: HMS Warrior 1860 *is seen here moored at Portsmouth Historic Dockyard where she forms a static exhibit.*

Miss Britain *is seen here on display in the National Maritime Museum, Greenwich. She is no longer in operational use but has been conserved indoors for visitors to enjoy.*

This page and facing page:
Motor Defence Harbour Launch Medusa *was launched in March 2010, following a major project to reconstruct her.*

especially if vessels are undercover and also ashore. In doing this, an essential part of their meaning, their mobility and the associated hands-on skills must be abandoned. The compensation will be the wonder and fascination of an authentic object, with all its human associations, that is not simply a representation of the past. The real thing should be inspiring and instructive for having survived from a time when design, purpose, technology and materials were not as they are now.

The conservation of historic vessels has come a long way in the last 30 years. The National Register of Historic Vessels (NRHV) and the National Small Boat Register (NSBR) are now available online, allowing conservation to take place against a clear picture of what makes up the quantum of historic vessels in the UK and crucially the 200 or so vessels which particularly reflect the rich maritime past of these islands and which form the National Historic Fleet. National Historic Ships has already published the first two volumes in this series *Understanding Historic Vessels. Recording and Deconstructing Historic Vessels* have provided a benchmark in best practise for maritime heritage, ensuring that all options are explored when a vessel reaches the end of its life and that the features which make a vessel significant are recorded and preserved for future generations.[1] *Conserving Historic Vessels*, published in printed form in view of the timeless nature of the conservation principles impressed within it, completes this series of guidance publications and will provide owners with the portfolio needed to ensure that their vessel is conserved in the manner which is most suited to her character, use and importance.

1. Kentley, Eric, Stephens, Simon & Heighton, Martyn, *Understanding Historic Vessels, Volumes 1&2: Recording & Deconstructing Historic Vessels* (National Historic Ships: London 2007).

HOW TO USE THIS BOOK

This book seeks to guide the vessel owner through the appropriate thought processes from first analysis of a vessel's significance to acquisition, further research and then to active conservation. At this point, the owner has reached the Conservation Gateway and an important decision must be made. The reader will be asked to consider the future use to which the vessel will be put and then to read the chapters appropriate to the answer. There is a fundamental distinction in how the vessel should be conserved, depending on whether operational use or fabric preservation is prioritised. Once this difficult choice has been made, the reader will be guided along the most relevant conservation route for their project.

Whilst it is recommended that the whole book is read at least once, it has been designed to allow users to follow a primary conservation route, or to come back at a later stage and pick out key points. Each chapter has a quick guide at the end and a navigation chart allows readers to see which sections are required reading, and which are related to a conservation choice. Look out for the nautical icons at the start of each chapter, which link to the book navigation and for the colour coding which marks the alternative conservation routes.

The book is intended as a practical guide to conservation ethics, but for those who want some extra background reading, there are separate sections giving a brief overview of conservation history, funding and tips on off-ship research, as well as case studies offering specific examples of the different conservation processes. Understanding the definitions of terms used in this book is very important; an alphabetical list of definitions is given after the chapter on maintenance. The end bibliography lists the key texts used in the production of this book. However, a number of these are no longer published and there are difficulties in locating further sources through recognised outlets or at all. Furthermore, conservation science is ever-developing and changing, so it is not wise to set down conservation practise in a permanent form. Therefore, National Historic Ships has created a dedicated web page at **www.nationalhistoricships.org.uk** which publishes downloadable documents linked to conservation. This is a valuable resource and new approaches, case studies, links to other key websites and the latest topical papers will be regularly added as a way of ensuring that the information supporting this book remains current.

HOW TO USE THIS BOOK

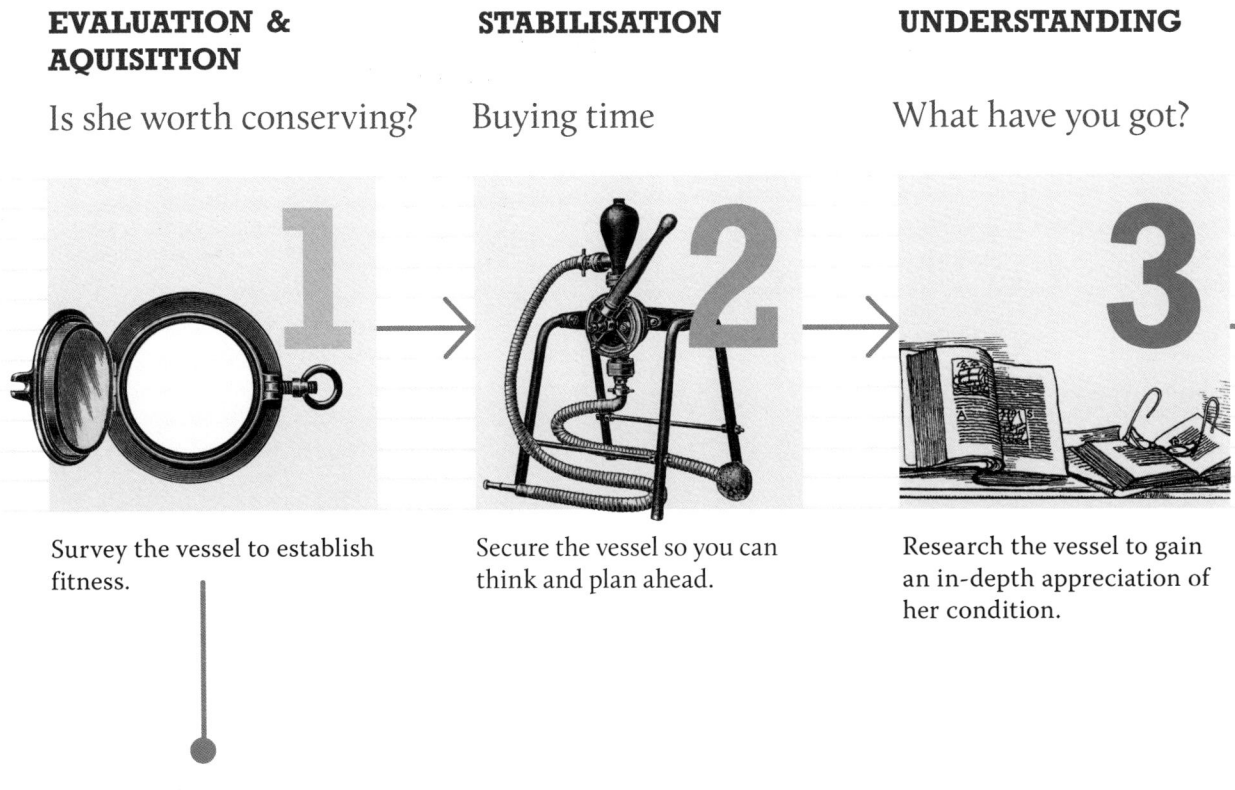

EVALUATION & AQUISITION

Is she worth conserving?

Survey the vessel to establish fitness.

If no, abandon project.

STABILISATION

Buying time

Secure the vessel so you can think and plan ahead.

UNDERSTANDING

What have you got?

Research the vessel to gain an in-depth appreciation of her condition.

ASSESSING SIGNIFICANCE

Why does she matter?

4

Establish if the vessel's importance merits conservation.

If no, abandon project.

THE CONSERVATION GATEWAY

Decision time

5

Decide which is the most appropriate route to preserve the vessel.

STATIC ASHORE
Full fabric preservation possible.

STATIC AFLOAT
Adaptations need to be designed to minimise fabric loss.

FABRIC ROUTE

OPERATIONAL ROUTE

PRIVATE
Adaptations need to be designed to minimise fabric loss.

COMMERCIAL
Adaptations need to be designed to minimise fabric loss.

HOW TO USE THIS BOOK

IS SIGNIFICANCE AT RISK & EVALUATING VIABILITY

What is happening to her?

Assess short and long term risks and carry out a feasibility study for conservation.

CONSERVATION PROCESS

Doing the work

Apply the conservation method(s) which are most appropriate to the vessel.

PRESERVATION BY RECORD

If conservation is not feasible, record and archive findings then deconstruct vessel.

REPLICATION

An alternative option?

If conservation is not an option consider building a replica using recorded data.

PRESERVATION

Preserve existing fabric and arrest deterioration.

RESTORATION

Return vessel to a known period with minimal new material.

RECONSTRUCTION

Return vessel to a known period using considerable new material.

ADAPTATION

Modify vessel for a proposed new use.

Apply your principal conservation process as determined by the route you have chosen earlier. You may also need to employ aspects of other processes for particular circumstances.

MAINTENANCE

Ensuring longevity

Implement a costed maintenance cycle at an appropriate level whether afloat, ashore, under cover or inside.

10 CONSERVATION PRINCIPLES

KEY CONSIDERATIONS

Historic ships & boats should be conserved according to their significance.

1

A small number of vessels have fabric of such high significance that they deserve preservation with minimal intervention to their fabric. Others are more suitable for keeping in or returning to operational use.

The aim of conservation is to retain the significance that has been identified and pass it on to future generations.

All aspects of significance should be dealt with in a considered and thoughtful way.

Rigorous maintenance is a key to good conservation practice for all vessels.

2

3

4

A formal statement of significance identifying and summarising heritage merit should be written for the vessel and regularly referred to during the conservation process.

This may mean that multiple periods of the working life of a vessel could have some significance worth preserving or presenting. Avoid the pitfall of assuming that conservation must date back to a particular time only.

An inspection and maintenance plan for the vessel needs to be devised at the outset of any conservation project. This applies equally to operating vessels or boats and ships in a museum. The plan should be properly resourced, monitored and changed if required, to make sure it is effective.

TEN CONSERVATION PRINCIPLES

Make and keep records throughout, including recording all changes to the vessel and what happened to any material which has been removed.

When in doubt, do the absolute minimum. Conservation demands a cautious approach to change.

Replace like with like wherever possible and practicable.

5   6   7

It can be forgotten that changes made during conservation should be recorded as carefully as alterations that took place before conservation.

Carry out a careful assessment before making any alterations. Once fabric is removed, the vessel's originality may be irretrievably impaired. All fabric that has been taken off the vessel must be

If similar materials cannot be sourced, the new materials introduced should be clearly distinguishable from the old.

If uncertain, don't do it.

affordable should be employed in all types of conservation.

8

9

10

A thorough understanding of the vessel's fabric must be developed at an early stage to avoid making inappropriate or unnecessary changes.

The skills of those invited to work on a project should be proven and matched with the project's needs. Ensure that experience gained from any project is appropriately and widely shared. Documenting and learning from decisions is essential.

Read this volume at least once before deciding which conservation route to adopt, then regularly refer to the guidance for the specific process chosen.

J.M.W. Turner's famous painting (1824) of HMS Victory at the Battle of Trafalgar (1805) illustrates the significance of this vessel which is one of the few of her size conserved for the nation and on display today.

A BRIEF HISTORY OF CONSERVATION

The vast majority of historic vessels built in the UK have disappeared for good or are known only through records. These records range from crude graffiti on a church wall to a full set of plans in the collections of the National Maritime Museum, the Science Museum and elsewhere. Complete surviving boats and ships built before 1800, whether afloat or ashore, are extremely rare. Fewer than ten complete vessels originating from the 18th Century are left. Most remaining 19th Century vessels were built after 1860 and represent only a fragment of all the categories of craft that were once sailed, steamed, punted, rowed, or towed. Most surviving historic vessels were built after 1900. If one is prepared to look far enough into the future, many of those that exist today will not survive and will be remembered only from whatever records we manage to make now.

Vessels, like other functional objects, were not designed for permanence, but to fulfil a particular purpose. Sometimes this was short-lived. Changes in the technology of warfare could make a warship redundant in a matter of years. HMS *Warrior* 1860 had an active naval life of thirteen years. The impact of the aggressive environment of the Atlantic or the North Sea on ocean-going traders gave them in the main a short lifespan. On the other hand, sound construction, continued usefulness, constant attention to maintenance and the availability of funds for careful repair could keep a small fishing punt, worked in relatively calm waters, in use for a century. There are some surprising examples of long life for vessels worked in hostile environments. When usefulness ran out, or was perceived to be outweighed by the cost of repairs, some vessels were adapted to a new purpose. Working vessels could be rearranged to carry a different sort of cargo or altered to a new form of propulsion. Naval and civilian vessels might be given a stationary second life, perhaps as a storage hulk, training ship, or houseboat. Vessels have been recycled into workshops, stores, or even rustic cottages, but their more likely fate was to be abandoned, burnt, or broken up.

Usefulness has always been the key to the survival of vessels. In the 21st Century, this is unlikely to be the same usefulness intended by the original shipwright, boat builder, or their subsequent commercial or private owners. Few categories of historic vessels on the water are used for the purpose for which they were first designed. Historic fishing boats, freighters and naval vessels are now used for leisure, education, as memorials, or have become part of the tourist industry. It is generally only vessels specifically designed for leisure which have their authentic purpose unchanged.

The survival of historic vessels which have a new operational use is governed as much by how adaptable they are to contemporary leisure or commercial use as by their intrinsic interest, though the two do sometimes coincide. Early surviving leisure vessels, yachts and motor boats are fortunate. As admired designs, they are considered worth the effort and expense of being kept in working order, in much the same way that vintage cars or old aeroplanes attract enthusiasts who will find the funds to take care of them. Some service vessels, such as dredgers, are less adaptable and therefore tend to be of interest to specific groups.

Size matters in boat and ship conservation. A vessel over 33 feet (10.05 metres) long is often reckoned to be beyond the repair and maintenance capacity of an individual private owner using a boat for pleasure, millionaires excepted. What can be done to conserve the really big ships is constrained by the near impossibility of manning them for operational or static use, and the difficulties of finding a place where they can be kept, within reach of visitors and with access to facilities and skills for maintenance.

Static conservation usually means that a vessel has found a new purpose as a public (though not necessarily heritage) asset and is made accessible to a wider audience rather than to a succession of private owners and users. Boats and ships kept in a static state are only a small percentage

A BRIEF HISTORY OF CONSERVATION

of surviving historic vessels. The earliest examples of the static conservation of ships reflect a wish to celebrate national prestige. In 1581 Queen Elizabeth I commanded that Sir Francis Drake's *Golden Hinde* should be preserved as a monument to his services and the glory of his country. The ship remained at Deptford 'as an object of curiosity and admiration' for about 90 years until she was too decayed to be repaired. Sound wood was then selected from her and made into a table and three chairs. One of the chairs was presented to the University Library in Oxford, the gift commemorated in a poem published by Abraham Cowley in 1668:

> '*Drake* and his Ship could not have wish'd from Fate,
> A more blest Station, or more blest Estate.
> For (Lo!) a Seat of endless Rest is given
> To her in *Oxford*, and to him in Heaven'. [2]

In the post-Romantic period, the national sense of history and heroism attached to Nelson's flagship at Trafalgar was not to be satisfied by conversion to furniture. HMS *Victory*, reputedly spared from being broken up circa 1830 at the insistence of the wife of the First Sea Lord, Thomas Hardy, was secured for the nation in 1921 as a memorial to Nelson and British naval power. The leading body in the campaign was the Society for Nautical Research (SNR), founded in 1910. It led the fundraising for the project and supervised her comprehensive reconstruction in dry dock at Portsmouth. The Society also campaigned for a national maritime museum, which was opened in 1937.

Small boats found their way into museum collections from the late 19th Century. The first were examples of what were then considered 'primitive craft', whether recovered ancient British log boats like the Dover Boat, Bronze Age vessels such as the 'Ferriby Boats', or small canoes and rafts from far-flung places, such as those in the former International Sailing Craft Association Collection. These illustrated a contemporary interest in ideas of progress and ethnography. British boats built after 1700, unless they could be identified as part of the 'primitive' tradition, such as coracles, attracted relatively little museum interest until after World War II.

In the 1930s, the SNR was far-sighted enough to recognise that regionally distinctive boats used by working people had cultural value and were disappearing at speed. Their Coastal Craft Committee, following pioneering work in Scandinavia, toured the UK coasts, measuring, drawing and photographing working boats. Along with parallel work published in *Yachting Monthly*, nearly a hundred designs, lines plans and arrangements were taken from existing craft. The drawing project did not continue beyond the great dividing line of World War II, but left a precious archive in the National Maritime Museum, Greenwich, with copy negatives kept in the Science Museum, recording many boats that have since been lost. More recently, and not before time, this 1930s work was used as the basis for *The Chatham Directory of Inshore Craft, Traditional Working Vessels of the British Isles*,[3] which is full of useful sources of further reading and information.

Most projects to make and keep actual ships and boats, rather than records of them, post-date World War II. Some types of working boat attracted the attention of individuals who banded together and raised funds to prevent them from disappearing. The Thames Sailing Barge Club was founded in 1948, encouraged by Frank Carr, then Director of the National Maritime Museum and was transformed into a Trust in 2003. The object of this group was to research and keep alive the skills of sailing and racing a very numerous type of barge rather than preserving them for static display. In this approach, there was an overlap in the transition from working boat to leisure craft. Some sailing barges survived in working use, others had been converted to working motor barges, whilst some were used for recreation, with all three functions in operation at the same time. 2,100 Thames barges were registered in 1910, more than all the historic ships that have been identified on the National Register of

2. Colin White, 'The Archaeology of Ships of War' in *Too many preserved ships threaten the heritage*, National Maritime Museum, Oxford University MARE, World Ship Trust, Nautical Archaeology Society, 31 October – 1 November 1992, Typescript.   3. Greenhill, Basil and Mannering, Julian, *The Chatham Directory of Inshore Craft: Traditional Working Vessels of the British Isles* (Chatham: London, 1997)

Historic Vessels (NRHV) as having maritime importance in 2010. Today there are about 30 Thames barges in operational leisure use. The Norfolk Wherry Trust was established in 1949 to buy and sail one of the last working Norfolk wherries. This was a type of boat whose purpose was replaced by railway development but which had proved adaptable to authentic leisure use, with an example of conversion for pleasure trips as early as 1863.

In 1952, a preservation society was formed to save the tea clipper *Cutty Sark*, built in 1869. The society, like the Thames Barge Sailing Club, was spearheaded by Frank Carr with the active support of HRH the Duke of Edinburgh. She was installed in a landlocked dry berth at Greenwich and reconstructed to her appearance as an active sailing ship. The Greenwich location and her proximity to the National Maritime Museum established her as one of the sights on the itinerary of tourists to London, seen by millions of visitors to Greenwich, with approximately 15 million visitors actually going on board between 1957 and 2006.

In 1969, the Maritime Trust was formed, again on the initiative of Frank Carr and with the support of the Duke of Edinburgh. It was amalgamated with the Cutty Sark Society in 1989.[4] The Maritime Trust acquired a number of ships for the nation. Other organisations, including museums, followed suit and made themselves responsible for looking after individual vessels. Some established museums added boats and ships to their collections, for example, The Imperial War Museum which acquired HMS *Belfast* in 1978, seven years after she had been saved by a preservation society. The Merseyside Maritime Museum took on the pilot cutter, *Edmund Gardner* in 1982 and the sailing motor schooner *De Wadden* in 1984. *Mary Rose*, raised from the bed of the Solent in October 1982, is the only recovered 16th Century warship with a unique collection of everyday objects relating to Tudor life. A number of other maritime and inland waterways museums, mostly independent, were founded from the late 1960s as a part of the boom in UK museums.

With the exception of the handful of small 'primitive' boats in museums, the endeavour to conserve historic vessels as public

Coracles have been conserved or replicated as examples of early primitive craft. These historic images show coracles in use, alongside a coracle model which forms part of the National Maritime Museum collection.

4. Littlewood, Kevin and Butler, Beverley, *Of Ships and Stars: Maritime Heritage and the Foundings of the National Maritime Museum* (The Athlone Press: London, 1998)

THE BURRA CHARTER

what have you got?

why does it matter?

what is happening to it?

what can you do about it?

who should be involved?

The 'boat club', based at the Scottish Fisheries Museum, is made up of a group of volunteers, who work together to conserve, maintain and sail Fifie herring drifter Reaper as an operational vessel.

assets is very recent and mushroomed in a 40 year period from about 1965. In the 1970s there was little understanding that museums and similar organisations would eventually have to compete with each other and with other tourist attractions for limited grant aid and visitor income. Some ship and boat projects were relatively well thought out and considered. Others were made in a spirit of enthusiastic heroism with little forward planning about the impact of environment and location on the sustainability of the vessels, with no clear idea of visitor numbers, and no assessment of how they would be financed in the long term.

The fate of individual vessels and collections dating from the late 1960s is an object lesson in just how important these considerations are to conservation. Few ships 'saved' as public assets in the 1970s and 1980s have escaped some sort of crisis of funding, management or location. The Maritime Trust's collection of historic vessels displayed at St Katharine's Dock was dispersed to other preservation bodies or into the private sector after it became plain that the collective maintenance costs could not be met. Many of the vessels needed major reconstruction by their new owners in order to put them back into good floating or working order. Boats now found in museums reflect collecting which was begun on the basis of what could be obtained, or what was donated, rather than a national or regional policy to secure the best or most representative selection for the future. This has left an inheritance of gaps and duplication, overlaid with problems of management and location.

Traditionally, those who care for historic ships have split into specialist groups. These often have expertise in a single type of vessel and support for their members or fellow enthusiasts but little sense of belonging to a wider heritage world. Specialist magazines, including *Classic Boat* and *Wooden Boat*, have helped to overcome insularity and connect specialist groups and private owners with one another. Heritage Afloat was founded in 1993 as a forum for owners operating vessels and, alongside European Maritime Heritage, worked to develop the *Barcelona Charter*,[5] a set of guidelines for the care and use of operating historic and traditional vessels. This book is particularly influenced by the *Illustrated Burra Charter*[6] which was developed specifically for Australian heritage and became internationally influential in the development of conservation charters and protocols. The *Charter* does not address the direct conservation problems of boats and ships, but the principles it recommends can be readily applied to historic vessels as a means of conservation planning. Kate Clark, formerly of the Heritage Lottery Fund, devised a simple set of questions which offer a short-cut to the heart of the *Burra Charter*:

What have you got?
Why does it matter?
What is happening to it?
What can you do about it?
Who should be involved?

This book seeks to make these questions relevant to anyone with a historic ship and help them to plan the conservation of their vessel as painlessly as possible and be in a position to do the best they can for her.

Whilst English Heritage, Historic Scotland, the Welsh Assembly Government (CADW) and the Environment and Heritage Service (Department of the Environment, Northern Ireland) have the authority, backed up by funding, to speak for historic buildings and structures in the different countries of the UK, until 2006, there was no single government funded voice to represent UK historic vessels. However, recognition that one collective body was needed grew as early as the 1990s, and as a result, the NRHV was drawn up by the National Historic Ships Committee, the predecessor of the Advisory Committee on National Historic Ships. The Register uses carefully established criteria to identify some 1,000 vessels over 33 feet (10.05 metres) long of historic maritime interest.

---

5. European Maritime Heritage, 2010, www.european-maritime-heritage.org 6. Walker, Meredith and Marquis-Kyle, Peter, *The Illustrated Burra Charter: Good Practice for Heritage Places* (Australia ICOMOS Inc: Burwood, 2004)

A BRIEF HISTORY OF CONSERVATION

It includes a group of approximately 200 vessels which comprise the National Historic Fleet, being of pre-eminent national significance and thus meriting the highest priority in terms of conservation. National Historic Ships also maintains the National Archive of Historic Vessels (NAHV) which lists over 400 vessels with historic potential, or which have been lost from the NRHV through natural wastage, sinking or demolition. More recently, the National Small Boat Register (NSBR) has been established as a parallel register, operating under the aegis of the National Maritime Museum Cornwall and has a database of more than 2,000 vessels.

CONSERVATION FUNDING IN THE UK & ABROAD

Funding shortages and sustainability problems are a common theme for everyone looking after historic vessels, whether they are in the private or public sector, in operational use or static exhibits. Boats and ships are expensive to maintain. In the 1930s Sir Thomas Lipton famously stated that simply owning and sailing a yacht was the equivalent to standing in a cold shower and tearing up £5 notes.

Considering the importance of the UK's maritime heritage, historic vessel conservation is under-funded by national government. Private owners, as is the case all over Europe, shoulder the main burden of financing their care and upkeep. A substantial number of ships on the NRHV are in private ownership. For boats under 33 feet (10.05 metres) long on the NSBR, the percentage is likely to be far higher. There are very few sources of grant aid available for the private owner apart from the small grants scheme administered by National Historic Ships and funded by the Department of Culture, Media and Sport. National Historic Ships is acutely aware that vessel owners need help in finding their way through the grant aid maze and has therefore published an online guide to funding sources.[7]

Historic vessels that are public assets in the UK fare badly for national support relative to some other countries. Mystic Seaport in Connecticut, USA supports over 80 historic vessels, benefiting, as do many American educational and cultural establishments, from substantial private donations, encouraged by attractive tax concessions. Nearer to home, Norway has a government minister responsible for its floating heritage, annual government aid and government-funded regional conservation centres where skills and facilities are available. In Denmark, the nationally-funded Roskilde Museum presents outstanding examples of recovered Viking vessels, along with replica vessels, which are regularly sailed. The Netherlands has some eight heritage harbours, a thriving industry in chartering and excursions on historic vessels and a system of loans at modest interest rates (for which there is hot competition) for private owners. France has begun to include ships and boats on its lists of protected monuments which makes them eligible for up to 50% of conservation costs, with the work requiring approval by the Inspectorate of Monuments.

With a tiny handful of exceptions (those under the ownership of national museums) historic vessels are not the direct responsibility of UK governments and therefore do not receive government grant aid. Only two hold any form of protection under current legislation. By contrast, listed buildings and scheduled ancient monuments enjoy well-defined levels of protection and have access to grant streams managed through English Heritage and the devolved administrations. Historic wreck sites have been subject to protection under certain circumstances since the 1970s: out of the 5,000 known wreck sites around the UK, 61 hold designated status. It is ironic that some of the most damaged vessels, known perhaps only from waterlogged fragments or the ghost of a hull imprinted in mud, have been looked at more carefully, and recorded and analysed more thoroughly, than ships with historical values considered worth presenting to the public.

7. National Historic Ships, 2010, www.nationalhistoricships.org.uk

HMS Belfast *is owned by the Imperial War Museum but still requires funding from external sources to conserve her. In 2010, London-based Russian companies financed work in recognition of her historic significance to their country through her service on the North Atlantic convoys to Murmansk.*

The question of whether the government departments responsible for heritage should be involved with historic vessels that are not wrecks has been debated, with concerns raised over the mobile nature of many UK vessels. National Historic Ships is promoting a system of spot-listing for vessels on the National Historic Fleet, to provide a breathing space for vessels at high risk whilst alternative options for their future security are explored. Until this scheme or something similar comes into being, the conservation of historic vessels, unlike buildings, historic landscapes and Scheduled Ancient Monuments is not subject to external legal pressures to undertake works based on published principles. With a tiny handful of exceptions, it is not illegal to destroy or alter an historic vessel, however important she is, as it is for a listed building or wreck site. Without statutory controls and associated grant aid, there is no encouragement for vessel owners to carry out a high standard of conservation in the same way that there is for the most important listed buildings.

Ships and boats kept under the umbrella of some museums may be supported indirectly by government funding, for example HMS *Belfast* via the Imperial War Museum, or the Merseyside Maritime Museum's collection of large ships (the steel pilot cutter *Edmund Gardner* and motor schooner *De Wadden*, both on public display in the Canning Graving Docks) and smaller preserved boats (currently in store), all of which are the responsibility of National Museums Liverpool. Museum ownership, however, does not guarantee adequate support, whether funding or skills-related. The resources of small museums, which may have no more than one or two boats, have to be spread across wide-ranging collections and some curators have little experience of how to treat, or best interpret large functional objects. In a complex 21st Century society connected electronically across national boundaries, including coasts, the maritime culture of the UK no longer has the impact it once had and needs more explanation than before. Ships and boats have ceased to be a familiar part of

A BRIEF HISTORY OF CONSERVATION

HM Submarine Ocelot *was launched at Chatham Dockyard in 1960 and later returned there after 27 years of active service for the Royal Navy.*

local and international travel at an individual level, although their economic importance has not decreased. Mainland Europe is accessible from the UK without seeing the Channel. Whilst 95% of all our imports arrive by sea, this has become an activity invisible to most of us. Museum interpretation today needs to address the discrepancies in what we know and appreciate of our maritime history.

For the private owner, or group of enthusiasts working on a vessel at their own expense, what is done to her is a matter of personal choice, using whatever advice can be obtained from immediate connections, articles scattered across a wide range of specialist publications and the internet. Some vessels in public ownership may qualify for grant aid from the National Heritage Memorial Fund, if they can demonstrate a 'memorial' aspect to the project. More substantial funding is available for museum and other vessel conservation projects via the Heritage Lottery Fund (HLF). This organisation has stood between many ships and the breakers' yards. Between 1995 and 2009, HLF awarded over £100 million to projects involving over 90 historic vessels. Grants are discretionary and it is mandatory that all projects seeking HLF funding help people to learn about their own heritage and that of others.

Organisations applying for Heritage Grants of over £1 million are required to produce a Conservation Management Plan,

She has been conserved as a static exhibit in the Historic Dockyard where she demonstrates the complexities of changing technologies in naval history.

and will always be asked for a detailed assessment of costs. Such documentation, along with a Business Plan, will involve a substantial amount of work and should be seen as an investment of thinking time and logical planning which will ensure that a project succeeds. It should convince not only the awarding body that the approach to conservation is sound, but also attract supporters (including potential trustees, volunteers, skilled enthusiasts and funders), as well as being a useful guide for contractors. It can be used later as a reference document for maintenance after the project has been completed.

For projects that involve capital and/or conservation work with a value over £200,000, HLF requires a costed Management and Maintenance Plan that clearly sets out what work and resources are needed to look after the asset over the next ten years. This process was introduced to avoid deterioration of good conservation over time, caused by unrealistic assessments of maintenance costs. HLF is also particularly concerned that applicants demonstrate how they will manage and maintain their heritage in the long-term.

In order to help potential applicants, HLF has published comprehensive guidelines online and in hard copy and it is crucial that anyone considering applying for an HLF grant consults these before starting their project.

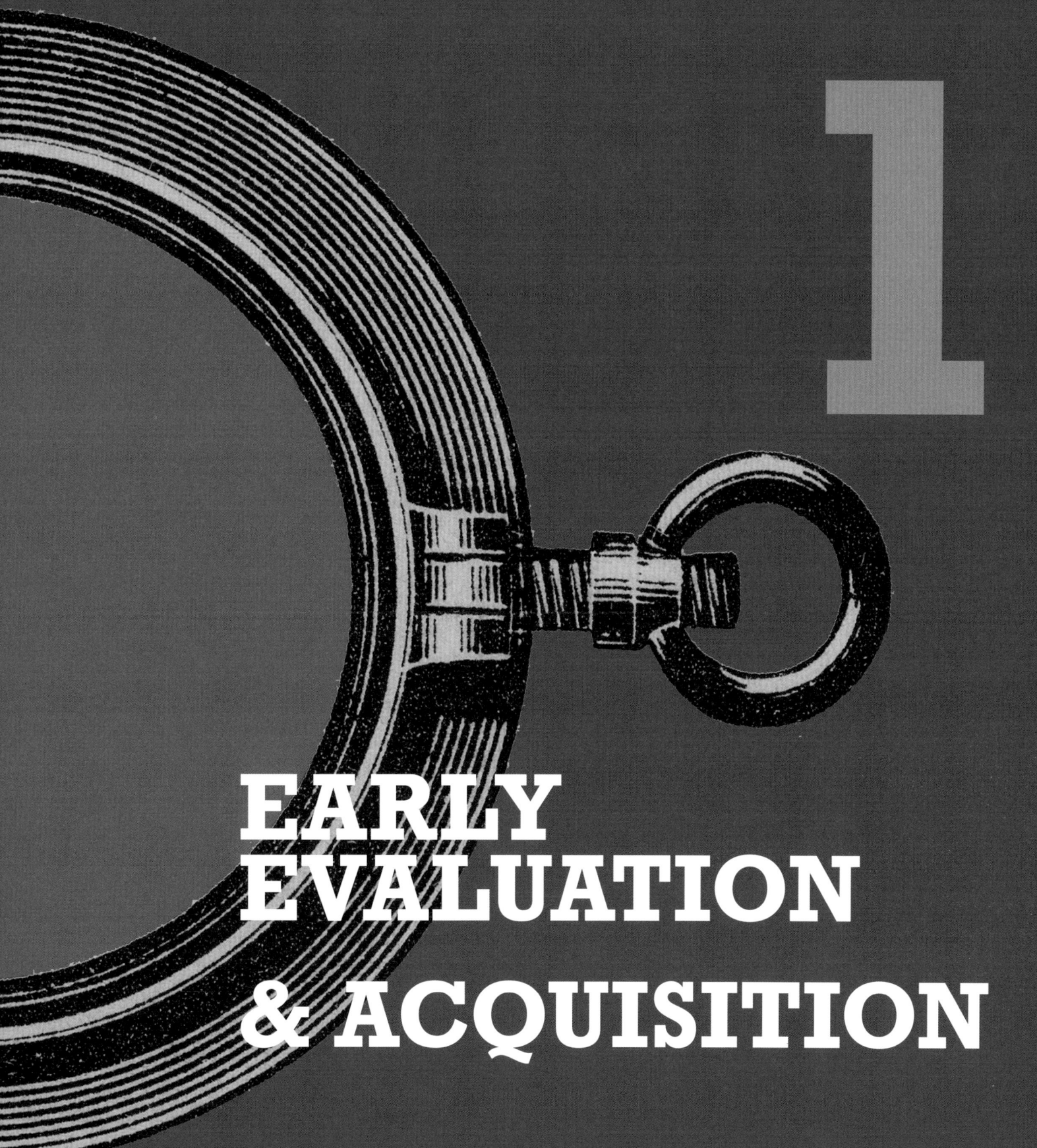

EARLY EVALUATION & ACQUISITION

1

EARLY VESSEL EVALUATION & ACQUISITION

Before acquiring a vessel, it is important to make an initial judgement as to her significance and whether her condition merits conservation in one form or another, rather than replication, recording or abandonment. This early assessment may be overturned later, but should precede acquisition, which brings liabilities.

Facing page: Sometimes, first sight of a vessel can be enough for an owner to fall in love with her. It is important to step back, analyse the significance of the vessel and think again about the demands a conservation project will entail before deciding to buy her.

Previous page: Coastal steamer, SS Robin. A vessel's significance, which may be identified through information about her working life, is critical to developing an understanding of whether she merits acquisition for full conservation.

There are likely to be early ideas about a vessel's future, especially when confronted with a boat or ship that seems on the brink of being lost for good. It may transpire on better knowledge that the first scheme is the best one, but equally it may prove not to be. Good conservation planning means a willingness to adjust or reject initial thoughts. All options and alternatives should be investigated and matched to the vessel as an understanding of her develops. Many well meaning projects have failed, with varying degrees of loss, due to insufficient planning time or stubborn devotion to an over ambitious or inappropriate scheme. For larger projects which need fundraising, it is good planning and logical judgement along with informed enthusiasm that will win support.

If a rapid assessment of significance, a condition survey or both, indicate that conservation of the vessel is not really viable a prospective owner is strongly recommended to abandon thoughts of conserving the vessel at this stage. The vessel can still be kept or adapted for other purposes, but the principles of conservation should not be applied. In many cases, there may not be time to assess the vessel in depth before acquisition. A quick analysis to establish the scope of the project can be supported by more detailed work later (see Chapter 4).

MAKING A RAPID ASSESSMENT

To quickly sum up a vessel's significance, it is best to start by writing down the different ways she is important. It may seem an obvious point, but with changes of name and registration, it is vital to make sure no mistake has been made

1

EARLY VESSEL EVALUATION & ACQUISITION

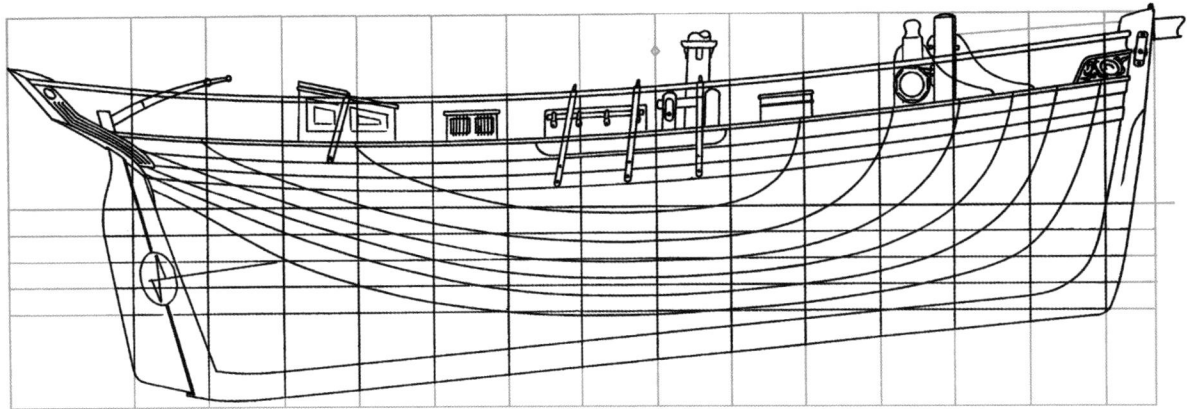

Information on the vessel's build, such as these plans, registration documents or photographs, can be useful aids to determining innovations in her design, aesthetic value and whether she is representative of her type and function.

when identifying the vessel. All craft on the National Register of Historic Vessels have to meet the following criteria, which offer a useful starting point of aspects to consider:

- What is the vessel's ability to demonstrate technological innovation?
- Is the vessel a good example of type (vessel design) and construction?
- Is the vessel a good example of a maritime function (purpose for which she was built)?
- Does the vessel exhibit a positive aesthetic impact?
- Does the vessel have historical associations with significant people, places and events?
- Does the vessel have significant socio-economic associations?
- Can the percentage of original fabric (with reference to that surviving at the end of the vessel's working life) be estimated?
- What is the vessel's age?
- How scarce are examples of this vessel type or construction?
- How scarce are examples of this maritime function?

A private owner, or an organisation, thinking of acquiring a vessel for conservation is well-advised to take some objective advice on significance. There is a danger that the prospective owner's heart may over-rule the head in terms of the vessel's value for conservation purposes. An expert on the vessel type or owner of a similar vessel should be better placed to give advice on how rare or exemplary she is. Contacts can be found through National Historic Ships, this organisation's Directory of Skills & Services published on the web[8], yacht clubs and associations.

8. National Historic Ships, 2010, www.nationalhistoricships.org.uk

1

A CONDITION SURVEY

A prospective owner's assessment and understanding will be immeasurably enhanced by a condition survey. However, it is best to target the survey at key elements of the vessel, especially if acquisition is a matter of urgency and there has been no time for detailed conservation planning. When time is short, an overall understanding of the likely budget required is vital, but too many concerns over detailed costing can be misleading or close down options. Remember, a professional marine surveyor will assess a vessel in relation to her intended future use. Therefore any surveyor must be carefully briefed to consider several different options for use against which to assess the vessel. The surveyor should look at the vessel's condition in relation to both fabric conservation and conservation for operational use. In many cases, the future use of the vessel will be clear, but in others, this may change as a full conservation management plan is developed. If it is obvious that she is destined for static display, there is no point in a condition survey that assumes she will be conserved to sailing condition.

The purpose of a condition survey at this stage is primarily to establish whether conservation is possible, and to exclude acquisition of vessels that are beyond saving. Investing the time to find the right people for advice pays dividends. Depending on the size of the vessel and the owner's experience and skill, a condition survey for a small boat might be undertaken by a prospective owner. However, on grounds of objectivity, it is advisable to find a suitably experienced marine surveyor, familiar with the vessel type and sympathetic to conservation. If her fabric is of outstanding importance, a marine conservator should advise on both condition and required stabilisation works. A structural engineer may be called in for advice about temporary support and repairs.

SS Robin, *seen here prior to the start of conservation work in 2009. The last surviving steam coaster from the 19th Century and therefore in the National Historic Fleet, she is being conserved as a static exhibit, displayed on a floating pontoon.*

ACQUISITION

Acquiring title to an historic vessel does not secure her conservation, it merely transfers ownership and, with it, liabilities. Whenever possible this should be delayed until a prospective owner has developed a conservation approach and planned out required fundraising. An existing owner may agree to prospective owners undertaking simple measures to protect a vessel at their own expense, or may be prepared to sign a legal option allowing title to the vessel to be purchased.

Both museums and private owners may be offered historic vessels *gratis*. This can be a double-edged sword, especially if they are offered by a patron or trustee of the museum. In the long term, accepting a vessel that does not fit with a rational collections policy may result in neglect, either of the boat in question or of other items in the collection which may have been disregarded to accommodate the maintenance of an unsuitable gift. Small museums without experience of the conservation of large functional objects should be extremely cautious in accepting an historic vessel before researching significance, relevance to existing collections and collections policies, conservation, maintenance and insurance costs in detail, as well as considering whether they can offer the right environment. Private owners being given a vessel for free should look beyond the emotional appeal and consider carefully the reasons behind the offer. The costs associated with accepting a vessel may be very high. Furthermore, private owners should question what they will do once conservation has been completed and ensure that a sustainable plan has been put in place.

Early evaluation of the Ladies Gig *revealed the need for immediate care and support to prevent further damage to the fabric. This revolving support frame was designed to minimise the risk of damage caused by over-handling, allowing the vessel to be turned 360 degrees by one person.*

EARLY VESSEL EVALUATION & ACQUISITION
a quick guide

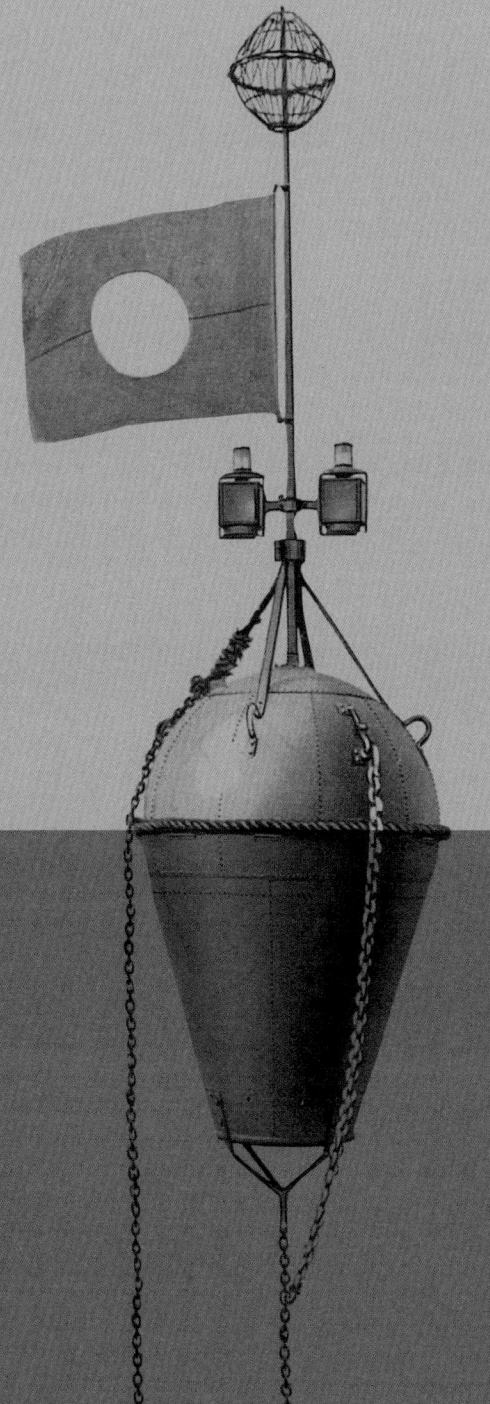

First, make sure the vessel has been correctly identified.

Acquisition should then be preceded by an early assessment of significance: 'why does she matter and to whom', accompanied by a condition survey.

This may have to be a rapid assessment and in-depth research will be mandatory later to ensure the vessel has been fully understood.

If possible, delay acquisition until conservation planning is further advanced.

When thinking of acquiring an historic vessel, remember to consider the demands which such a project will place on the owner, owner's family or the organisation, including conservation, maintenance and insurance costs.

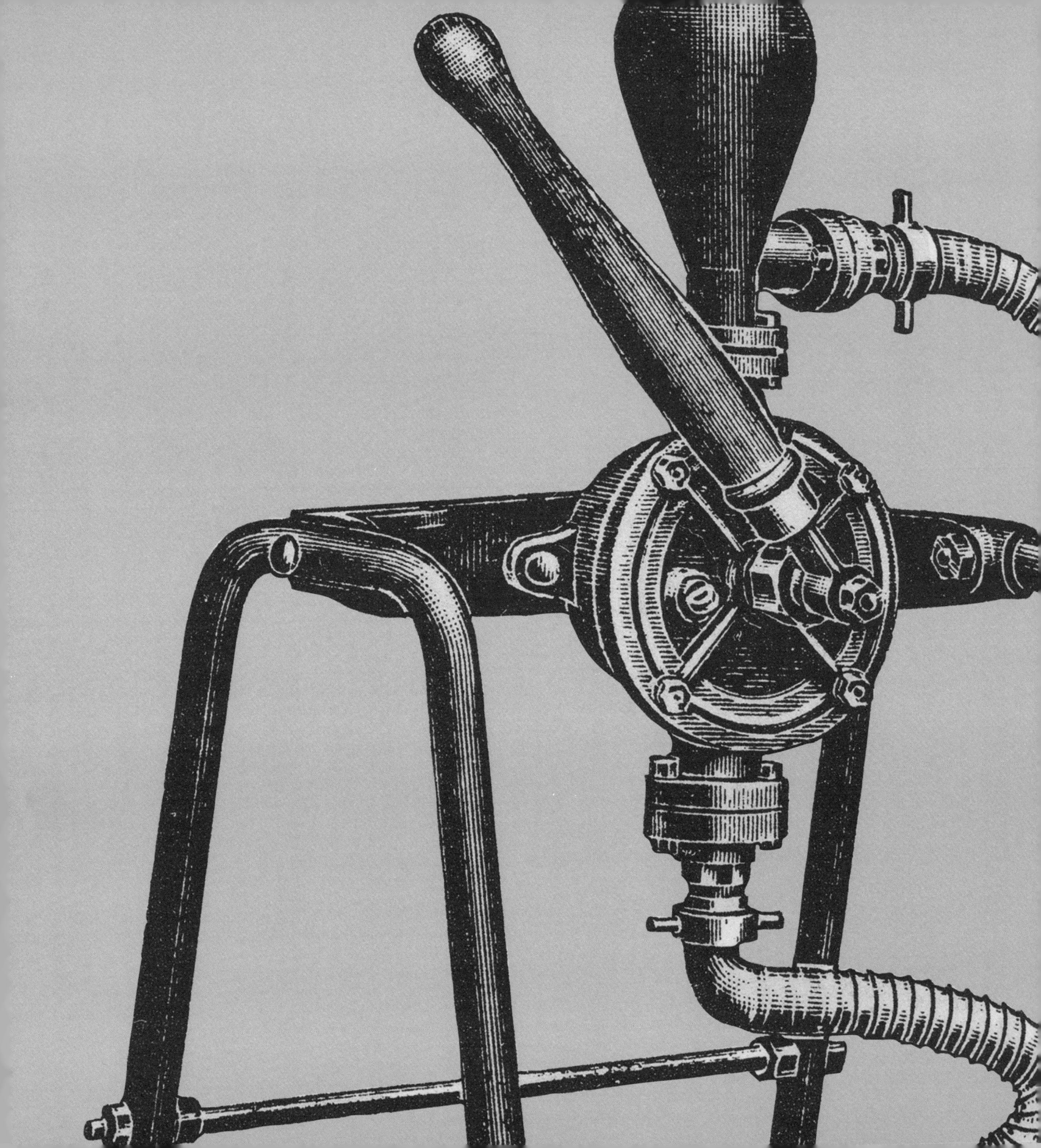

2

STABILISATION

Buying time 2

STABILISATION

Stabilisation is an important way for the vessel owner to win some thinking time, knowing the fabric of the vessel is temporarily secure. However small the boat, or complex the ship, all conservation benefits from reflection in advance of acquisition.

Above: Thames barge Edith May *under the protective covers which were used to keep her in a stable condition, prior to carrying out major reconstruction work due for completion in 2010.*

Previous double page spread: Jhelum *was a merchant sailing ship built in Liverpool in 1849 which was declared unseaworthy and abandoned in the Falklands in 1870. Targeted measures were undertaken to prolong her life to enable full recording of the hull.*

The expense needed to conserve an historic vessel generally far exceeds initial expectations and it is worth trying to get it right first time. If immediate anxieties about the condition of the vessel can be temporarily set aside, this will create a breathing space. In this time, detailed information about her condition and history can be gathered (see Chapter 3), her significance properly assessed (see Chapter 4) and the viability of conservation analysed, all of which can often take longer than anticipated.

For vessels whose owners are seeking a grant from the Heritage Lottery Fund, a period of stabilisation is essential. Applying for funding is a lengthy process during which a vessel can seriously deteriorate. If the application is not successful, and other funding cannot be found, a stabilised vessel is easier to pass on to another organisation, to consider for an alternative project, or to be recorded before she is broken up. This chapter looks at the fundamental elements which must be taken into account when stabilising any historic vessel.

A PROTECTED ENVIRONMENT & MAKING TEMPORARY REPAIRS

Most importantly, the vessel should be kept in an environment where she is protected from general depredation, theft, fire and vandalism. In the case of floating vessels, a shore-based electricity supply is desirable. It is easy to underestimate the time needed for stabilisation works and it is wise to explore prospects for an extension of stay. For private owners, the nearer the boat is to them, the better. Travelling distance is a disincentive to getting on with work that may be dull but remains essential.

Adequate physical support must be provided in conjunction with good access for work. If the vessel is in the open air, protection from rainwater (which can be one of the greatest short-term threats to a wooden vessel) needs to be devised. It is worth constructing a roof over the vessel to protect her, which will also allow for work to be carried out underneath. Good ventilation at all times is crucial and needs to be designed to avoid jeopardising security or letting in rainwater. Temporary covers must not be in conflict with the need for ventilation.

Preventative measures should be taken to avoid wet and dry rot breaking out in wooden vessels ashore. Wet and dry rot flourish in humid conditions but diminish when humidity is reduced. Raising the temperature artificially in sealed compartments by just two degrees can halve the relative humidity and help to protect against rot, but must be balanced against the need for ventilation. Experimentation with heat sterilisation, whereby the temperature of the vessel is raised to some 40°C, has proved to be successful in the prevention of wet rot. However, such an approach will be limited by the type and size of vessel to be conserved. Stand-alone dehumidifying machines can be helpful in regulating conditions. It is important to recognise that over-dehumidification can also cause damage. Therefore the vulnerable material should be assessed, along with the surrounding material and the level of dehumidification controlled according to need in order to avoid shrinkage or embrittlement of the fabric. If moisture content of wood is below 15%, fungal growth is unlikely.

With every vessel, deterioration of materials should be identified, investigated and remedied when possible. Electrolytic corrosion is caused by stray electric current; galvanic corrosion is caused by the interaction of dissimilar metals. Both can be helped by the use of anodes. In vessels permanently ashore or in dry dock (particularly iron and ferrous-fastened wooden vessels) chloride contamination of iron or steel can continue to be a problem even if the vessel is indoors or under a cover. The cause of active rot and rust should be removed first, then treated with appropriate chemicals and a record kept of what is done. Depending on the circumstances, propping and temporary repairs may be appropriate. In exceptional cases, conservation is first aid alone. The life of hulks can be extended by measures to protect them from weathering and tides. This will slow down an inevitable demise and may give an opportunity to learn more and disseminate knowledge by recording. It will be of interest that the British Navy was concerned with the whole issue of stabilisation in the first quarter of the 19th Century. This is reflected in a publication by John Knowles, Secretary to the Committee of Surveyors of His Majesty's Navy.[9]

A good illustration of stabilisation as first aid is provided by the merchant ship *Jhelum*, built in Liverpool in 1849, then left anchored at Port Stanley in the Falkland Islands in 1870 'in a foundering state'. A 1984 survey recommended targeted and robust first aid work to prolong her life by supporting the bow area, shoring up the starboard side, strengthening the starboard splash zone and repairing the roof. Initial work was undertaken by volunteers from the 1st Battalion, the King's Regiment, the local Liverpool

A survey carried out on Box Boat 337 *concluded that whilst the majority of her hull was stable the two lower side planks needed replacing, as did the keelson, if the vessel was to be conserved for operational use. Her owners – the National Waterways Museum – decided to stabilise her out of the water pending securing the funding and materials necessary to conserve her. The Box Boat was lifted out and rested on chocks, covered over by tarpaulins to protect her from the weather. Her planks were marked with chalk to indicate where the work was needed.*

9. Knowles, John, *An Inquiry into the methods which have been taken to preserve the British Navy* (London, 1821)

STABILISATION

Above and facing page: Morecambe Bay Prawner, Helen II *being moved to Conway where she is undergoing conservation. It is important to think carefully before lifting a vessel, to make sure she will be supported properly during the transfer and that appropriate measures are taken to prepare her new location prior to arrival.*

regiment, with subsequent consolidation carried out by staff from the Merseyside Maritime Museum, who also carefully recorded her. In this way, *Jhelum* was stabilised with the works monitored and maintained over subsequent visits by the same museum staff. She was assessed as a significant vessel, but not unique and much reduced in importance by her poor condition, which made full preservation not a viable option.

There are inexpensive and effective methods of basic care, such as ventilation and weather protection that can be employed by any owner when stabilising a vessel, such as providing covers, clearing the interior of rubbish, and gentle cleaning; recording fittings *in situ*, then labelling and storing them if removed. However, depending on the complexity of the vessel and her condition, first-aid and temporary repairs in order to stabilise the vessel may need a professional shipwright or conservator.

MOVING THE VESSEL

In some cases, the environment where the vessel lies may not be suitable for stabilisation and the owner will have to consider moving her. If she is at risk, presents a risk to other vessels or needs first aid that can only be done ashore, she may need to be moved, or hauled out. This decision requires careful thought as a boat can be damaged beyond repair during moving, exacerbating existing problems or even breaking her back. There may also be safety risks for the people involved in the move and it may be best to hire or, better still, acquire the voluntary services of a suitably qualified professional. Whether or not to move, how it should be done, and the extent to which help and advice should be sought, is a matter of judgement and experience. A suitably qualified marine surveyor, and a boat yard or crane hire may be needed. Spreaders must be used and appropriate support for the keel provided if a crane lift is involved. Before moving a vessel, a photographic record should be made of anything likely to be at risk, as well as a note of how the vessel lies in the water (whether she is afloat or submerged) and where spot loadings such as engines or hull strong points like internal bulkheads are placed. The level of record will vary between projects, with the priority being any vulnerable or delicate parts of the vessel. Once stabilised, there is more time to undertake targeted recording.

Moving may require dismantling parts of the vessel to lighten her. Any vulnerable items which might get damaged or put her safety at risk during the move should be photographed, removed, labelled, and carefully stored beforehand. A list of what has been taken, where from, and how it was attached must be made and kept safely. All loose

2

objects should also be part of this process. If a boat needs moving, it is not advisable to do this alone, however small and light she may seem to be. Always ensure after moving a vessel that she is well supported beneath the keel, and shored as required. Paul Lipke gives good advice in 'Choosing the Best Moving Method for You'.[10] Depending on the size and the fragility of the vessel, help may be sought from other owners who have been through similar experiences.

OBSERVATIONS

If a likely use has already been identified for the vessel, it may have an impact on how she is stabilised. If the boat or ship is destined for static display, whether afloat or ashore, treatment of her fabric will differ from a vessel intended for operational use. In either case, it is important to take advice from people with the relevant skills and experience and brief them fully about the project aims.

At this stage in any conservation project, the owner should be endeavouring to carry out the minimum work required to ensure stabilisation. The aim is to slow down deterioration that puts the vessel at risk in the short term, rather than to embark on a conservation route which has not been fully planned. Once any causes of deterioration in the vessel have been identified and further decay temporarily halted or alleviated, the owner will be in a position to assess the project and make sure that the best conservation process is being adopted.

10. Lipke, Paul, Spectre, Peter and Fuller, Benjamin (eds), *Boats: A Manual for Their Documentation* (Museum Small Craft Association, American Association for State and Local History: Tennessee, 1993)

If the vessel is not in a safe location, is at risk from the elements or in a position where practical first aid cannot be achieved, it may make sense to move her.

STABILISING THE VESSEL
a quick guide

2

Stabilise the vessel by temporarily securing her fabric as close to the condition when found as possible.

Ensure that the keel is well supported along its length and that shores are placed solidly as required to bilges, and also to stem and stern overhangs.

Protect the vessel from rain ingress and maximise ventilation to all spaces.

Make the minimum intervention into her fabric and don't get carried away – the aim is to retard decay, not carry out ad-hoc restoration or reconstruction.

If possible, do not replace fabric to avoid structural failure at this stage. Careful, reversible propping, clamping and splinting support is preferable until conservation planning is complete.

If the vessel has to be moved in poor condition, make the decision with care and think about the physical risks.

Inspect the vessel regularly to maintain stability, particularly when a project takes longer to start than expected.

Record any interventions that have to be made and avoid inadvertent loss of historical evidence e.g. stripping paint may lose evidence of historic colours.

Costs incurred in stabilisation will be irretrievable if conservation turns out to be unfeasible, but these are likely to be negligible compared with the price of failure at a later date.

3
UNDERSTANDING

OFF COWES.

3

What have you got?

UNDERSTANDING

The right decisions about conservation cannot be made without a real understanding of the vessel in question. This means finding out not only about the history of her fabric but the story of her whole life. If a vessel is no longer operational, this includes her original life at sea, as well as what has been done to her and what activities she has been involved in since. It is very important to put aside all previous assumptions and look at her again with fresh eyes. This chapter explains how to learn more about the vessel, both through the materials of which she is composed and through alternative off-ship sources.

FABRIC RESEARCH

Previous page: Three yachts are shown racing off Cowes, Isle of Wight, 1923. They are believed to be Britannia, Terpsichore *and* Ilyrica. Britannia *(left of centre) was King George V's racing yacht and won 23 out of 26 races entered that year. King George left instructions that she be scuttled after his death, which was duly done. When the vessel no longer survives, historic images such as this become even more valuable to our understanding of her today.*

The tale of an historic vessel may be told simply through her fabric. Just as with building conservation, there is no substitute for careful observation of a boat or ship: the more informed the observation and analysis the better. There will be information in the fabric of the vessel that is not available from any other source. This can be more reliable than data from either paper documentation or oral history. A historic written or drawn record may refer to work that was proposed, but perhaps not executed, or carried out differently. Oral history is of great value and can fill gaps that no written document can plug, but the human memory can be faulty. The ideal way to collect oral history is to record it and transcribe the record in full. Oral history may be transformed and corrupted by omission or elaboration especially if one person is recollecting, not what they knew themselves, but what they were told at second hand.

The value of fabric analysis can be seen in the case of the 19th Century frigate, HMS *Trincomalee*, where documentary evidence indicated that she had been re-coppered at a certain point in her lifetime. However, careful examination of the nailing pattern when the coppering was removed showed that it was in fact largely original, with repairs confined to the waterline. Close inspection of the vessel's fabric had resulted in two interesting discoveries: the survival of her coppering, but also a new understanding of the term 're-coppering' which may refer to patching up only.

3

The most accessible way to make observation permanently useful is to take photographs of the vessel. The first step should always be to obtain a good set of photographs, which move logically around the exterior and then through the interior and are carefully labelled. Photographs should include a whiteboard giving the vessel name, date, caption and direction of view. Every detail is potentially important, however dull it may appear. These photographs can prove to be really useful later on and can be enhanced by being lit with a good flash gun. It is important to use some method (for example a measuring rod or, with a large scale feature, a person) to indicate the scale of what is being photographed. It can also be valuable to film a vessel in a structured way so that the inter-relationship between each element and the craft is recorded. One example of this is the filming of ss *Great Britain* in the Falkland Islands and her return voyage in 1970 by the BBC Chronicle team. Measured drawings are even more helpful.[11] The extent and level of these will be determined by the available skills and funds, but they should not be regarded as a luxury. Producing drawings by hand measurement is the most effective way of getting really acquainted with a vessel. Good drawings and simple sketches can be annotated and used in a host of different circumstances. They can be copied and marked up as part of a works contract or used to record changes that are made during conservation. A set of fair copies as well as those showing changes can be hugely helpful to future owners.

A careful examination of all fabric should establish the particulars of the vessel's initial design, materials, construction, propulsion, arrangement and details of her finish, along

Below: It is important to analyse the fabric of a vessel carefully, looking to see what can be learnt from it. Fabric can provide information about the way the vessel was built, historic boatbuilding techniques or can demonstrate changes of use to which the vessel may have been put at different points in her life.

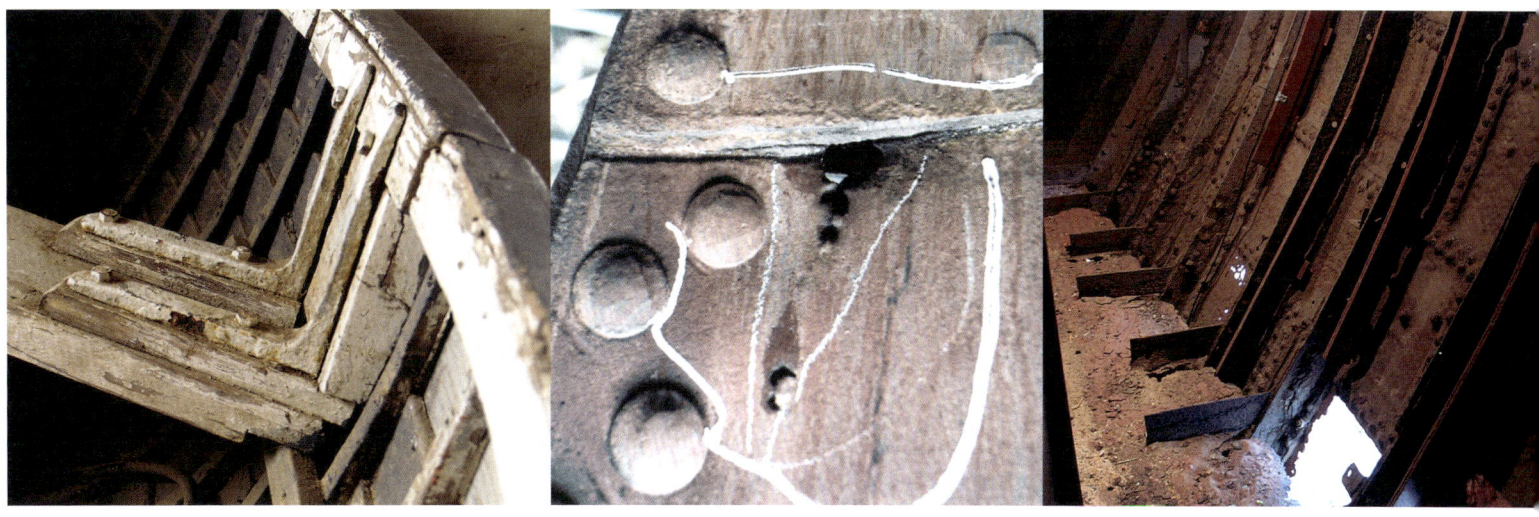

11. Kentley, Stephens & Heighton, *Recording Historic Vessels* (2007)

UNDERSTANDING

with information about any changes. These might be evidence of refits, maintenance, periods of neglect and any damage suffered. It is always worth looking round with someone else with a good knowledge of the vessel or other vessels of the same type, and creating a conversation or dialogue with them. Any features that are difficult to understand should be carefully noted and should merit a photograph, sketch or measured drawing.

It can be helpful to divide the vessel up into elements:

1. Hull; decks; structural members; deckhouses and superstructure; hull and deck openings (including evidence of fastenings and finishes). In the case of wooden boats in particular, it is important to identify the type of metal fastenings used.
2. Interior spaces including: cabins; holds; compartments; trunks and passageways with associated joinery, trim, furnishings, fittings and finishes.
3. Equipment including: masts and spars; rigging; boats; deck equipment; provision for fishing nets, armament etc.
4. Machinery; tankage and piping; electrical equipment; mechanical systems.

Facing page: HM Frigate *Unicorn, of 46 guns, was built for the Royal Navy in Chatham Dockyard and launched in 1824. She is seen here at her berth in Dundee, where the Unicorn Preservation Society is looking at options for long-term stabilisation and conservation.*

It may prove more of a challenge to tease out what has been done to a vessel's fabric since she has been in a museum, or used as a visitor attraction, than to uncover changes when she was in operational use. Observation and investigation, combined with oral history may be the only sources of information for this phase. Puzzles or queries that arise from observation and analysis may need off-ship research to solve. For example, patented elements in 19th Century ships, or the composition of coatings may provide valuable dating evidence. The frigate *Unicorn*, built in 1824, has preserved numerous shipwright marks on her timbers. These have now been analysed in a doctoral thesis and have helped to explain not only the methods of naval shipwrights, but the story of timber acquisition and management at Chatham in the 1820s.

Observing and analysing fabric can be undertaken by any owner, particularly for smaller vessels, but it is always worth collaborating with someone who has expert knowledge of the type, or the vessel herself. For large complex ships, the required skills may be found in a suitably experienced naval architect, shipwright, maritime conservator or maritime archaeologist. The latter, who may have extensive experience of diving on wrecks, should be quick to spot evidence of changes in a vessel's fabric. National Historic Ships may be able to help in finding an elusive expert.[12] Notes, sketches and measured drawings should be dated and titled, always giving the name of the vessel and the name of other people involved.

12. National Historic Ships, 2010, www.nationalhistoricships.org.uk

3

UNDERSTANDING

OFF-SHIP RESEARCH

The second way to learn more about the vessel is by off-ship research, which can often bring to light history that cannot be gleaned from the ship's fabric. An old photograph may show a form of rigging or a finish for which all the physical evidence has disappeared and which could then be re-instated. This may be 'paper history' only, but research might indicate a problem with her initial design or open up a phase of her operational life that was previously unknown.

With increased digitisation, freedom of information and popularity of genealogy, there are many sources available which the vessel owner can look into personally. Owners who have never undertaken research before often find it a great pleasure, very rewarding and compulsive. A private owner may be better motivated to go the extra mile, or better placed to spread research out across a period of time than a professional researcher. When owners are new to research, it is important to remember to reference sources used. A brief account of the project published in the right journal or magazine can generate information from readers who have known the vessel in the past. A website with an e-mail address can attract offers of material from all over the world.

If little is found about this particular vessel, some gaps can be filled by investigating others of the same kind and sourcing line drawings of a sister ship or similar vessel, or good quality drawings of the construction and details of contemporary vessels. In some cases, research proves addictive and it is necessary to remember that some lines of enquiry are less important than others and can be put on hold until later. Each angle of research should be assessed in terms of its relevance to the vessel's conservation. Some research, like the personal histories of the crew in a merchant ship, will be superfluous at this stage. However, if the crew members or previous owners are still alive and elderly, it may be prudent to interview them now. Sources which are likely to yield maximum information for minimum time, effort and money should be looked at first, with plans and drawings likely to be the priority.

Research should be relevant to conservation and cover the written, graphic and oral history of the vessel. The following questions are a good starting point. They will need to be developed accordingly for each vessel:

1. Who designed and built her, when, where and for what purpose?
2. What are her construction materials and fastenings?
3. What was her sequence of owners and users?

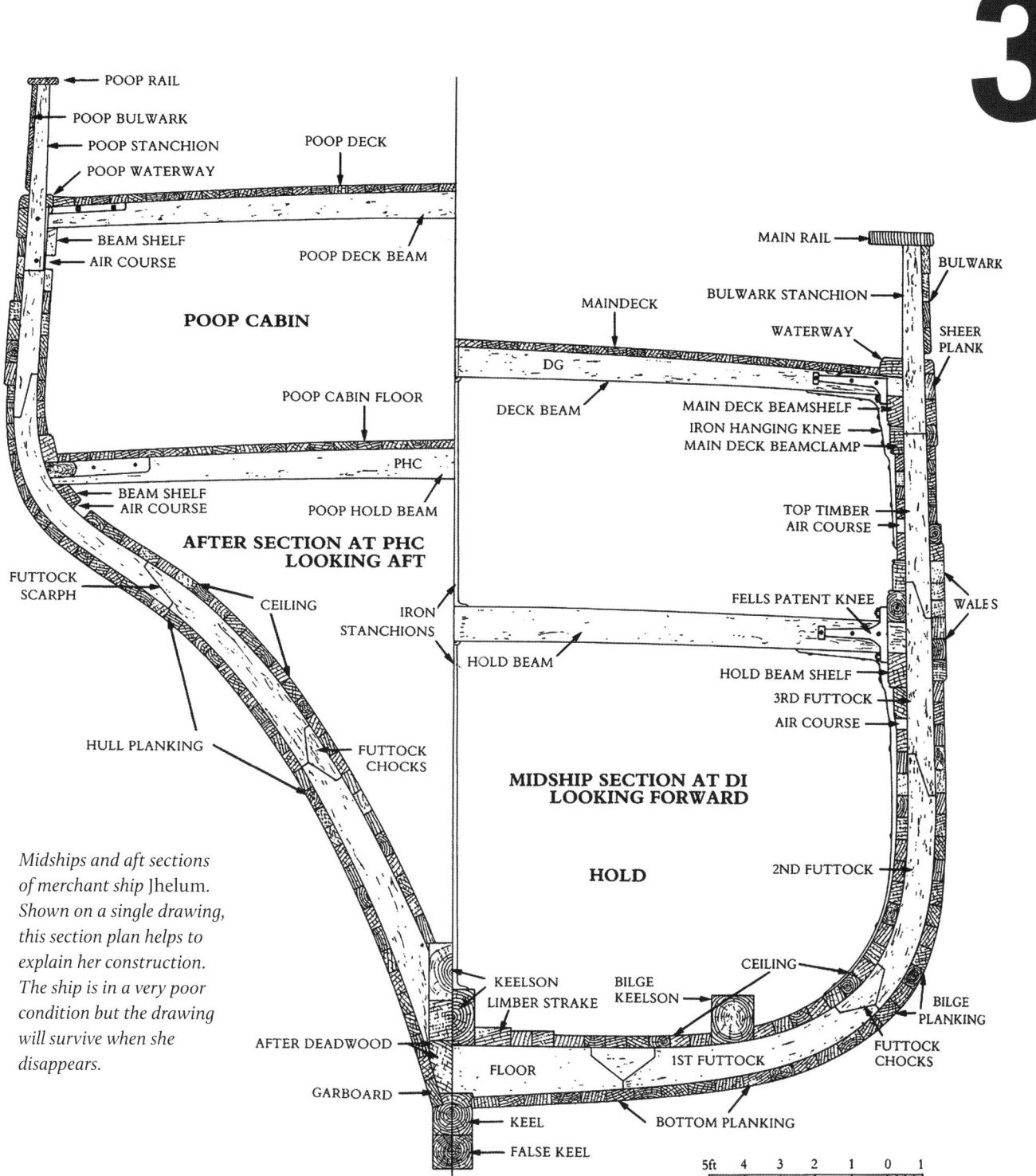

Midships and aft sections of merchant ship Jhelum. Shown on a single drawing, this section plan helps to explain her construction. The ship is in a very poor condition but the drawing will survive when she disappears.

4. How was she used?
5. What was the impact of changing use on her fabric?
6. Does she have a history of associations with different people or groups of people? (This might range from association with a particular boat club, to a local fishing industry or people whose ancestors emigrated in her).

The discoveries made in any off-ship research should be written down and fully referenced so the item can be followed up again. Notes should include the name of the archive, the document reference number and the website or place in which the information was found. The information on websites is often updated and it is useful to include the date at which they were visited. The author, title, date and page number of any publication used should be noted. The source and, if known, date of any photographs or other images should be given. The name of any individuals offering oral history should also be listed, preferably with contact details and the date they were visited.

Every effort should be made to keep a copy of research material in a separate place, in case one set goes astray or is accidentally destroyed. Private owners who have spent a lot of time on research finding useful old photographs or drawings should pass the originals on to the next owner with the vessel and keep copies. A good set of referenced research material and photographic records of the vessel may well enhance her value at any future point of sale.

OBSERVATIONS

A good understanding of a vessel can be achieved in a concentrated programme of work in which her fabric is carefully examined and analysed and off-ship research is undertaken. However, it is also common for the fabric of a vessel to become gradually better understood over time, especially when partial dismantling reveals new information. Similarly, new research sources can turn up, or existing research may need to be developed during a project. It may turn out that more information is needed to better understand materials and methods, and a different set of off-ship sources will then have to be examined. It is important to keep notes and reports up to date with new understanding and to make sure that old reports are clearly marked 'superseded' when this is the case, to avoid confusion.

Both strands of research – observation and analysis of fabric and researching off-ship sources – require formation of records. The level of record will depend on available

Above: A print of a barge being repaired on the foreshore at Bermondsey in the early 20th Century, by artist and engraver James McBey.

Facing page: This vessel, towering over a group of workers' cottages in Millwall in 1919, illustrates the type of historical associations which link vessels to certain social groups, individuals, places or events.

Watercolour showing the deck of the Cutty Sark *being replaced at the East India Dock, 13 September 1954.*

resources, but must always be well referenced so they can be used easily by anyone at a later date. When off-ship research has been completed, it is then important to cross-check what has been found against the analysis of surviving fabric. An effective way of doing this is to develop a timeline for the history of the vessel covering both strands of research. For example, if she had a refit at a particular date, can evidence of it be found in her fabric? If there are elements of her fabric that seem to be part of the same phase of alteration, can they be linked with what has been found from off-ship records and dated? If there are elements in her fabric that are unexplained by any off-ship research, consider all the options as to why they are there and test out the most likely answer. The conservation principles set out by English Heritage offer helpful guidance in understanding and articulating the wide range of values (evidential, historical, aesthetic or communal in origin) which apply to heritage assets.[13]

13. English Heritage, *Conservation Principles, Policies and Guidance* (2008), www.english-heritage.org.uk

UNDERSTANDING THE VESSEL
a quick guide

3

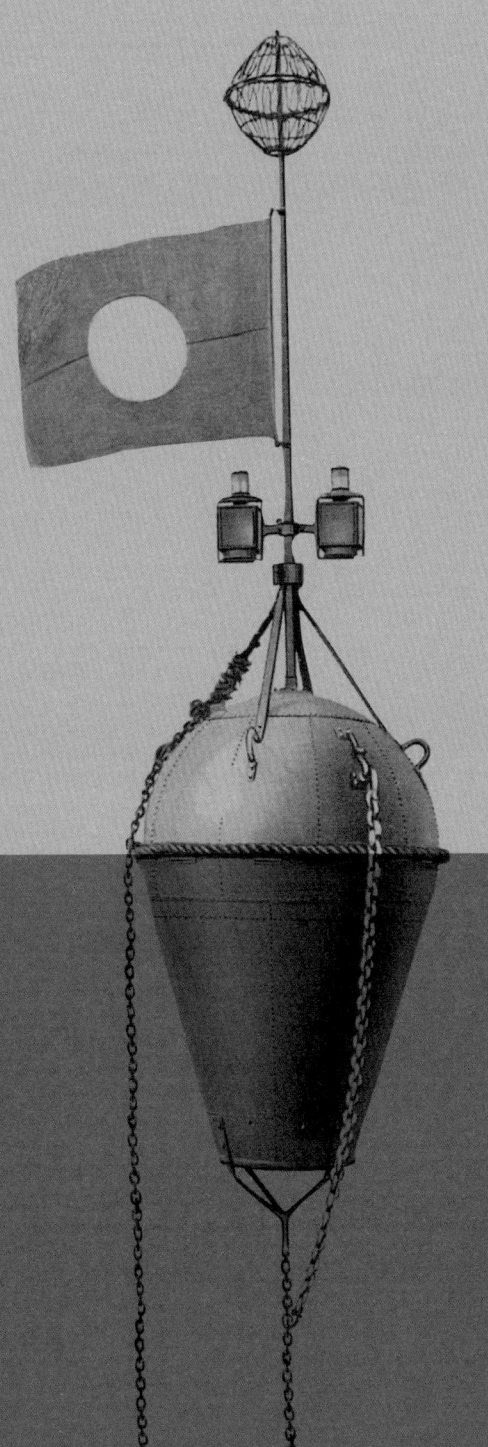

Don't start working on the vessel, other than emergency first aid to stabilise her, until measures have been taken to develop a thorough understanding of her.

Understanding involves:

1. **careful observation and analysis of existing fabric**
   - **Taking and interpreting photographs**
   - **Creating measured drawings**

2. **off-ship research into other sources**
   - **Locating relevant oral, documentary and pictorial material about the vessel's history.**

Bear in mind that not all off-ship sources are equally reliable.

Make sure all the information found is cross-checked against the surviving fabric.

Use clear references so research can be re-visited by future generations.

RESEARCHING

RESEARCHING AN HISTORIC VESSEL

Sources for off-ship research vary from vessel to vessel, according to size, function and special characteristics. The ss *Great Britain*, for example, generated intense contemporary discussion in 19th Century journals of engineering and her engines were important enough to be recorded in detailed scale drawings of 1845.

Smaller working craft are likely to have left fewer primary records in archives than ships, and research should make use of information in print. Publications on working boats include helpful illustrations and photographic records of vessel types associated with different working locations.[14] This is a quick overview of the key sources, but more information can be found by visiting the online bibliography for this publication.

Plans now held by the National Maritime Museum which show the hold of the broadside ironclad HMS Warrior *1860 and the ship's inboard profile.*

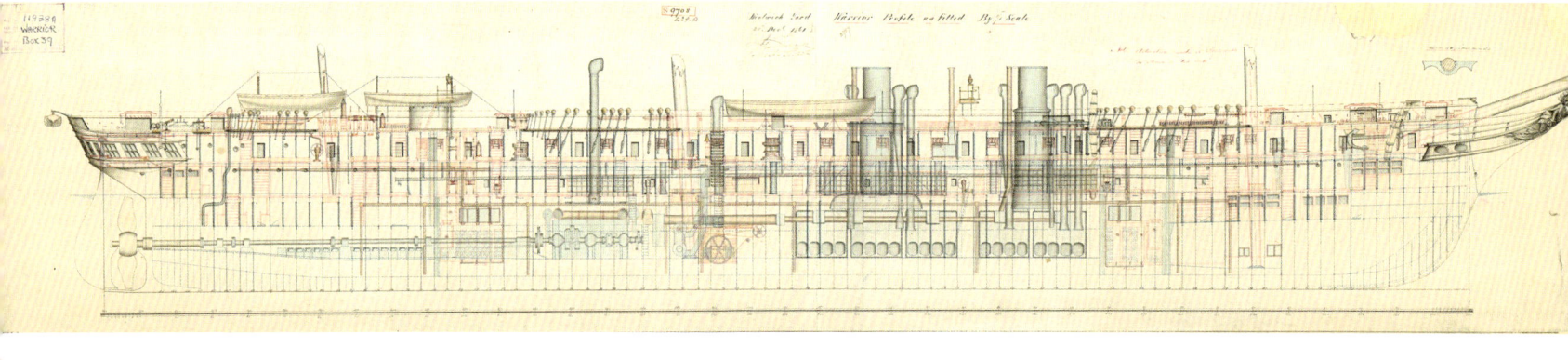

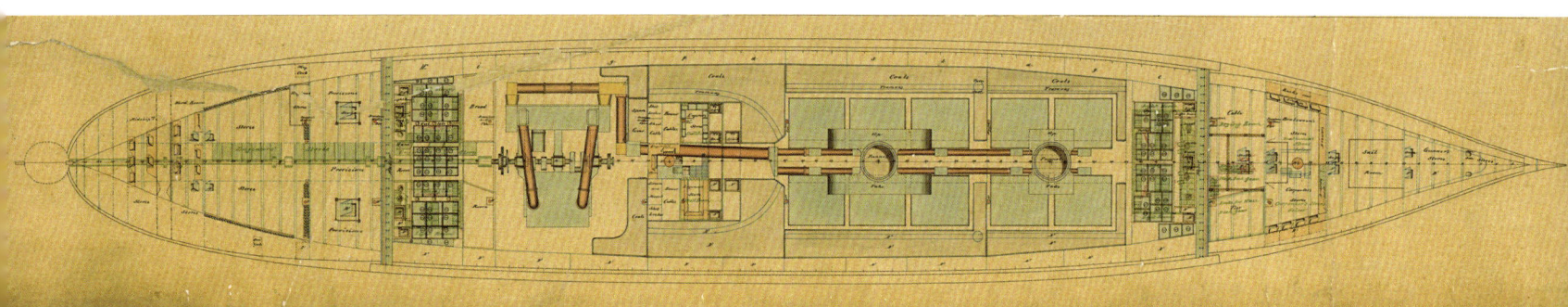

14. McKee, Eric, *Working Boats of Britain: Their Shape and Purpose* (Conway Maritime Press: London, 1983)

A shipbuilder's model of the cargo vessel, Framlington Court *(1924), made entirely in wood and painted in realistic colours. The fittings include a pair of anchors at the bow, bilge keels, a companion ladder, a single four-bladed propellor, anchor winches, ventilators and lifeboats. The level of detail shown here demonstrates the value a contemporary ship model can have when developing an understanding of a vessel. This can be critical if subsequent changes to the vessel's hull or fittings render the model the sole source of information on her original specification.*

RESEARCHING MERCHANT SHIPPING

The first starting point for any owner researching a British merchant vessel is to check for her details in *Lloyd's Register of Shipping*. This is an annual list of merchant shipping published from 1764 to the present day. It should provide a specification of the vessel including such details as: official number, type of vessel, master, dimensions, engines, survey, age, build and owners. A complete run of these Registers is held at the National Maritime Museum and other similar repositories. If *Lloyd's Register of Shipping* can not be found, an alternative source might be the *Mercantile Navy List*, started in 1851.

Lloyd's ship survey reports, covering the years 1833-1945, are also held at the National Maritime Museum. The Registry itself at Tooley Street holds other technical records and plans of certain classed ships. A rival to Lloyd's Registry existed in Scotland – a classification society called the British Corporation for the Survey and Registry of Shipping, serving mainly Scottish-based shipping. Its records of hull and machinery, survey reports and plans, circa 1891-1949, are held in the Business Record Centre at the University of Glasgow. Another possible source for information on individual ships is lifeboat call out records, which often list vessel names.

Having established some basic technical details about a vessel, the owner may then wish to know more about where it sailed. For this, *Lloyd's List*, a newspaper reporting shipping movements and casualties should be consulted. This runs from 1741, with an annual index from 1838-1927. Copies are held at the National Maritime Museum from 1779 onwards. Many shipbuilding firms have gone into liquidation, lost their records in a fire, or simply not survived. However, some of them still exist and have wonderful archives, whilst others have sent their documentary

Print of the Temeraire, *104 gun ship, lying at Rotherhithe in September 1838, prior to being broken up.*

15. Ritchie L.A. (ed.), *The Shipbuilding Industry: A Guide to Historical Records* (Manchester University Press: Manchester, 1992)
16. National Maritime Museum, 2010, www.nmm.ac.uk
17. Knight, R.J.B., *A Guide to the Manuscripts in the National Maritime Museum* (Mansell: London, 1980)
18. Mathias, Peter, and Pearsall, A.W.H., eds., *Shipping: A Survey of Historical Records* (David & Charles: Newton Abbot, 1971)
19. National Maritime Museum, 2010, email: plansandphotos@nmm.ac.uk
20. Colledge, J.J., *Ships of the Royal Navy: The Complete Record of all Ships of the Royal Navy from the 15th century to the Present*, Volumes I & II (1970, 1989, partly revised edition, 2003)
21. Lyon, David, *The Sailing Navy List: All the Ships of the Royal Navy – Built, Purchased and Captured – 1688-1860* (Conway: London, 2001)

material to the local record office. It is worth checking *The Shipbuilding Industry: A Guide to Historical Records* which lists all the principal shipbuilding collections, their content, type, availability of material, technical, photographic, plans and the repositories where they are held.[15]

If the vessel was owned by a major shipping company, this will be identified by the entry in *Lloyd's Register of Shipping*. The next step is to find out whether or not this company's records survive as they may be a rich source. They could be held by various repositories around the country. The National Maritime Museum website lists all those companies whose records are in their collection.[16] The very useful *Guide to the Manuscripts in the National Maritime Museum, Volume II* is a good introduction to the records of shipping and shipbuilding industries held by the National Maritime Museum.[17] There are also substantial archives of shipping trade industries held at the University of Liverpool, the Merseyside Maritime Museum, in Glasgow, Hull, Edinburgh and Newcastle. *Shipping: A Survey of Historical Records* is unfortunately now out of print and also out of date, but contains a very good description and listing of the shipping records in county and other record offices.[18]

A key part of any conservation project will be the location of original plans and drawings for the vessel if these survive, as well as historic photographs. The National Maritime Museum holds the largest collection of these. Their historic photographs catalogue is searchable online, but it is necessary to e-mail the ships plans department[19] to find out whether they have any material on the relevant vessel. A major incident or event in a ship's history could have been published in the national or local press. *The Times* Digital Archive can be consulted by an online keyword search, free of charge at the Guildhall Library. Other newspapers, including local papers nationwide, can be viewed at Colindale, the British Library's newspaper archive.

RESEARCHING ROYAL NAVY SHIPS

When researching Royal Navy vessels, there are a number of published sources which are good places to start, such as JJ Colledge's *Ships of the Royal Navy: The Complete Record of all Ships of the Royal Navy from the 15th century to the Present*.[20] The other great work of reference is *The Sailing Navy List*, Volumes 1 & 2.[21] Another source found at the National Maritime Museum are the records of the Director of Naval Construction, including the Admiralty Ships Covers, with very detailed content on relevant design and construction details of individual warships or classes of warships built between the 1860s and 1939 and the records of the Navy Board, including ships' contracts and technical specifications for ships built in commercial yards for the Navy from the 17th to the 20th Centuries. *The Navy List* runs from 1782 to the present day and gives details of ships in the Royal Navy. Copies are held at the National Maritime Museum and National Archives. The National Maritime Museum also holds a world famous collection of Navy Board models from 1655-1715.

RESEARCHING YACHTS OR SMALLER VESSELS

Using the same technique as described in merchant shipping research (above), the private owner should start with a search of *Lloyd's Register of Yachts*. This was published annually from 1878 to 1980 and is an invaluable reference for details of pleasure craft, although owners had to pay to be included, so the Register is not comprehensive. Similar to *Lloyd's Register of Shipping*, it provides a specification for each vessel with details of construction, dimensions and ownership. From this, it is possible to build up a complete list of owners and location of any listed vessel throughout her history. Copies of this work are held by the National Maritime Museum, other key repositories and many yacht clubs.

Other information on the vessel can be gleaned from old yachting magazines. These are very useful, particularly where a key event is known which might have been published at the time, such as date of build or launch, change of ownership or race winning. Key magazines to consult are: *The Yachtsman*, *Yachting Monthly*, *Yachting World*, *Classic Boat*, and *Practical Boat Owner*. Comprehensive collections of magazines and journals are held by the National Maritime Museum, the Bartlett library at the National Maritime Museum Cornwall, yacht clubs and other major archives. Some magazines date back to the late 19th Century. It is worth contacting yacht clubs in the area the vessel was located at different points during its lifetime to see if the owner (identified from *Lloyd's Register*) was a member. Yacht club archives vary, but some like The Royal Yacht Squadron or The Royal Cruising Club have excellent libraries with lists and photographs of members and their vessels. The Royal Yachting Association website has a complete list of existing UK yacht clubs.[22] However, the archivist must be contacted to arrange an appointment before making a visit.

There are a number of early sources for photographs of pleasure craft. A key place to begin searching is the archives of Beken of Cowes – marine photographers since 1888 in the Solent. Beken's website allows the user to make an email enquiry to see what material has survived.[23] Another source, the Kirk Collection which dates from the 1920s, is also held in Cowes and again is worth checking. The Francis Frith Collection brings together images as early as 1860 and has some wonderful views of fishing ports and harbours at that time, although it is often impossible to identify individual vessels.

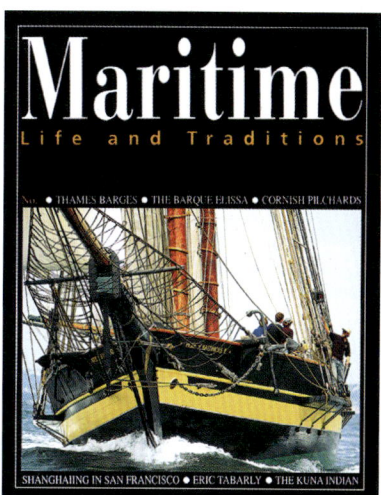

Yachting magazines such as Maritime Life and Traditions *can be a valuable aid to off-ship research. Remember to check the letters page and news sections, as useful snippets of information on individual vessels which would not be found anywhere else can sometimes be located here.*

22. Royal Yachting Association, 2010, www.rya.org.uk

23. Beken of Cowes, 2010, www.beken.co.uk

4

ASSESSING SIGNIFICANCE

Why does she matter?

ASSESSING SIGNIFICANCE

Understanding the various ways in which a boat or ship matters to people is the touchstone for making all decisions, large and small, about how she should be conserved. This is the difference between conservation, where the owner makes the significance of the boat or ship a deciding factor in what is done, and a project where the owner rebuilds or adapts an historic vessel simply to please him or herself.

A well observed and researched understanding (see previous chapter) is the only basis for analysing significance. A vessel may matter for many different reasons. She may be a rare surviving example of a type or remarkable for technological innovation. Conversely, the existence of other vessels of this type may lessen her significance. The vessel may retain an exceptional percentage of original fabric. She may have played a special role historically. She may have a particular relationship with a place or a group of people.

The first chapter of this book recommended an initial rapid assessment of the vessel under 10 headings. However, now that the more detailed fabric analysis and off-ship research has been carried out, the significance of the vessel will need to be looked at in greater depth and then formalised in a written statement of significance. This is particularly important when funding is being sought. Sometimes it can be difficult to look objectively at a vessel and analyse what is special about her. This chapter offers guidance on how to achieve this and the key points which must be considered in each case.

MAKING AN IN-DEPTH ASSESSMENT

Previous page: ss Great Britain *was designed by Isambard Kingdom Brunel and is seen here on her launching day, 1843, in Bristol. At this time, she was the largest ship in the world, over 100 feet longer than her rivals, and the first screw-propelled, ocean-going, wrought iron ship.*

Working from the initial assessment, the owner should look again at the reasons why the vessel is significant. To do this, it may be necessary to add to the off-ship research already undertaken. A good model to use is James Semple Kerr's concise publication, *The Conservation Plan*,[24] which offers guidance on conservation planning at all levels, although not specifically for historic vessels. As with Kerr's model, categories of significance should be tailored to each project. There is no universal standard for assessment that can be applied across the board. If it seems obvious that the vessel matters for a particular reason, this should not be omitted just because it does not appear on a published 'how to do it' list. Equally, it is easy to neglect areas of significance if the

24. Kerr, James Semple, *The Conservation Plan* (National Trust: New South Wales, 1996)

people who are making decisions are not interested or experienced in those aspects. Kerr offers a universal approach to assessing significance by developing the following set of questions which simplify and ease the process in a reasonably objective style:

1. WHAT IS THE VESSEL'S ABILITY TO DEMONSTRATE HISTORY IN HER PHYSICAL FABRIC?

This asks the owner to think about the importance of the vessel herself as evidence. The evidence must survive physically to be considered under this heading. One way of sub-dividing 'ability to demonstrate' is by thinking about what surviving evidence there is for designs, functions, techniques, processes, styles, customs and habits, or uses and associations in relation to events or persons. How early, intact, or rare these features are may also have an impact on a vessel's significance. One of the most memorable examples of physical evidence is the shot holes from the 1805 Battle of Trafalgar which can still be seen in the fore topsail of HMS *Victory*. Kerr points out that check lists have limitations. For instance, these may fail to prompt the owner to consider the importance of the evidence of wear and tear on a vessel's hull. Yet this can have a strong emotional or scientific interest for the public, highlighting the working life of the vessel and impacting on the conservation approach which is adopted.

The fore topsail of HMS Victory, *which survives from the Battle of Trafalgar, is seen here being conserved by a team from the Textile Conservation Centre. Extensive holing is thought to be a result of musket and cannon fire during the Battle. A long gash through the linen is believed to be caused by the mast of HMS* Victory *as it smashed to the deck. The sail has now been surface cleaned using low-powered vacuum suction in combination with soft brushes and statically charged cloths to remove particulate soiling.*

ASSESSING SIGNIFICANCE

Facing page: Vessels which played a key role evacuating the Allied forces from Dunkirk in 1940 are still remembered for this today, with the 70th anniversary in 2010 seeing some 50 of the surviving vessels returning to the Normandy beaches. This connection with British history makes these vessels significant in a way that could not be appreciated purely through their fabric or design.

2. WHAT ARE THE VESSEL'S ASSOCIATIONAL LINKS FOR WHICH THERE IS NO PHYSICAL EVIDENCE?

Links of this kind may often arise from the working life of a vessel. A small fishing boat may be connected to a particular local family or community, or have long associations with a boat club. All the surviving Dunkirk Little Ships are important for the role they played in Operation Dynamo, whether or not this is evident in their fabric. However large or small the vessel, it is helpful to think of all the different constituencies of people who might have an interest in her, either now, or in the future, and why she may be important to them as well as to the owner. Historians of engineering appreciate that the ss *Great Britain* matters for the technical innovations of her original design, including their impact on modern ship-building. They may not appreciate that, refitted as an emigrant ship, she is a critical part of the family history of thousands of Australians who are descended from the passengers she carried to Melbourne between 1852 and 1871, that Trollope wrote one of his novels on board, or that she carried the English cricket team for one of the early international cricket tours of Australia. This information, which is all part of her significance, is not attached to physical evidence developed from the ship's fabric, but came from off-ship research. It is also important to consider wider vessel links, such as those with places, particular ports, shipyards, trades, industry and, in some circumstances, known wreck sites.

3. HOW DOES THE VESSEL'S SHAPE OR FORM COMBINE AND CONTRIBUTE TO HER FUNCTION?

To assess the significance of a vessel's design, it is important to consider not only her lines and how these made or make her fit for purpose but also the materials she was built from, her overall aesthetic impact and her setting. Whether she remains in her original working environment, or creates an emotional effect will also add to her significance.

Some answers to the above questions may be more important than others. It is essential to rank the different areas of significance so that an understanding of the conservation priorities is developed. However, be aware that a graded system can have its disadvantages. It is easy for the levels of significance to be misunderstood, encouraging unnecessary neglect or even removal of elements considered to be of lesser worth.
A separate category of items that are additions or anachronisms from outside the working life of a vessel is a supplementary approach upon which decisions on re-installation, storage or disposal can be made.

4

SUMMARY OF A CONSERVATION PLAN

1. Agree the aim of the plan & how it will be used

2. Understand the ship
   Gather physical & documentary evidence

3. Co-ordinate & analyse evidence
   Involve all stakeholders

4. Assess & state significance
   [exceptional – considerable – some – little]

5. Gather information
   Requirements for retention of significance
   Physical condition
   Requirements for feasible uses
   Develop detailed management and maintenance actions,
   including a business plan outlining costs
   External requirements

6. Develop policy
   Explain how the vessel will be managed

7. Evolve strategies & options for implementation

8. Monitor & review the plan

4

The autobiography of a vessel, told through her fabric, should consider all phases of her life, rather than simply her original build. Later periods can be a key part of her story and may be interesting in their own right. Material from these often survives better and can be of greater importance than her original form. It is bad conservation practice to ignore significant changes and adaptations. If there is very little left of the vessel 'as built' to conserve and the value of later phases is neglected, unnecessary and damaging reconstruction can follow.

RRS *Discovery* was built in 1901 for the National Antarctic Expedition and had a major re-fit in 1923-1925 before being used for marine research, including groundbreaking work on whale stocks and oceanographic studies. This research represented an important phase of her history and the coincidence of significant surviving fabric with a particularly interesting period of her purpose led to the decision to restore her to this timeframe rather than her 1901 design. The earlier era and her association with Scott of the Antarctic have been covered in a purpose-built visitor centre.

RRS Discovery, *seen here on the stocks, is now displayed as a floating static exhibit in Dundee. In 2004, the Dundee Heritage Trust commissioned a full structural survey of the vessel, drawing up a conservation plan for her future care. An award from the Heritage Lottery Fund is now helping to stabilise the vessel, whilst key areas in need of attention are conserved.*

OBSERVATIONS

An honest assessment of significance may mean changes of mind and recognition that the vessel is not as significant as first thought or is significant in different ways from those originally identified. In the case of a private owner who has fallen in love with a boat this may not matter. However, if grant aid is essential, her significance will be one of the keys to obtaining it. In this circumstance, it is better that the owner reluctantly acknowledges that the vessel is less significant than originally hoped and abandons the conservation approach. No individual is likely to have a fully rounded view of why an historic vessel matters and collaboration in assessing significance is highly recommended. It is helpful to have some external advice from another vessel owner or professional with a strong interest, to avoid personal attachment clouding judgement. An outsider's review of a written statement of significance offers a useful balance to check this tendency. For Trusts producing a formal Conservation Management Plan, future decision making will be far more effective if a range of interested parties can reach a consensus on significance. Where volunteers play an important part in the life of a vessel, they should be invited to contribute, but commissioning a specialist to prepare the plan may also draw out aspects of significance that would not otherwise have been identified. There are obvious advantages in asking as wide a circle of local people and communities as possible for their views, perhaps by putting on an exhibition and inviting comments. If the setting of a static vessel is important, asking the Local Planning Authority for a comment on a draft of significance may alert them, for the first time, to the ship as an important part of local as well as maritime heritage.

The passenger liner Aquitania *(1914) in the Gladstone Graving Dock, Liverpool, in preparation for her maiden voyage across the Atlantic. The scale of the ship can be clearly seen in this view taken from the bottom of the dock, which shows the hull plating on the starboard side.*

ASSESSING SIGNIFICANCE
a quick guide

4

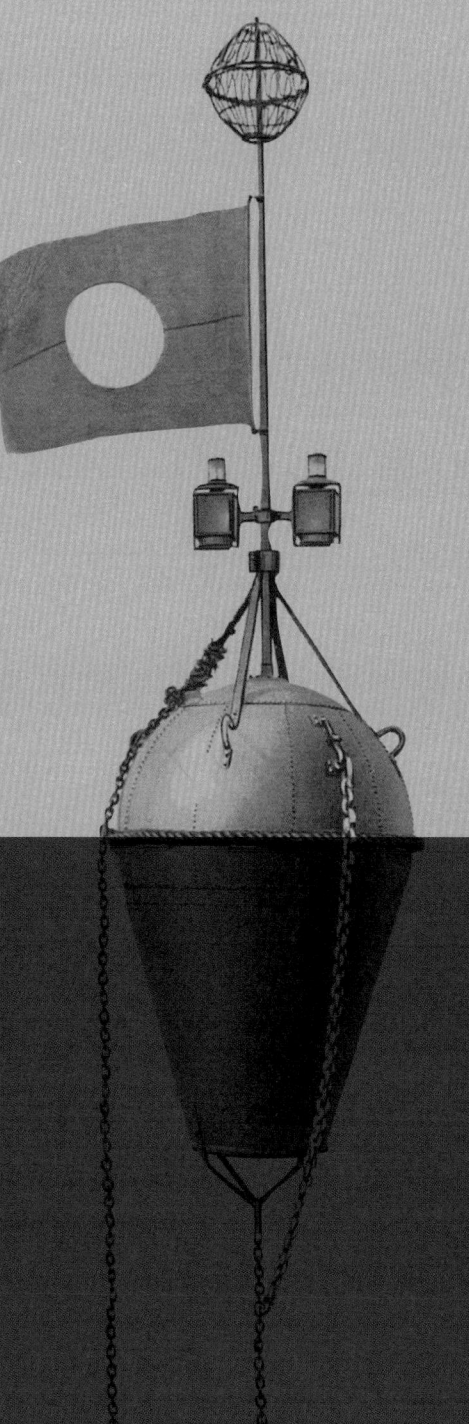

A vessel's significance should be the principal guide to the conservation route adopted and the decisions taken on her future use and management.

Significance should be assessed broadly, recognising the importance of a vessel to different groups of people and acknowledging different points of view.

If significance is ranked in order of perceived importance, it does not mean that aspects judged to be of lesser significance should be automatically neglected or removed.

A vessel of any age is likely to be the product of changing phases, not just her original design. All periods of her life should be carefully assessed for their significance.

If there is very little left of the vessel 'as built' to conserve and the value of later phases is not properly recognised, unnecessary reconstruction will follow.

CASE STUDY | M33 | STATEMENT OF SIGNIFICANCE

M33

M33 is a naval monitor, designed in 1915 and not particularly significant in terms of naval architecture or ship construction, while her naval career after 1919, although of passing interest, does not support her case for permanent conservation with any force. But in her wartime service between 1915 and 1919 she possesses very strong credentials which make her eminently worthy of consideration.

ABILITY TO DEMONSTRATE

In her relative ordinariness, she is a representative survivor of the smaller type of naval vessel generally employed for everyday wartime work. Designed, in effect, as a floating gun platform for a particular if limited wartime purpose, she could be risked close inshore off hostile coasts. In this capacity she provided valuable gunfire support to the armies ashore, and in other routine patrol and blockade duties she relieved more versatile ships, such as destroyers, for deployment in active roles. Lessons learned from the experience of the monitors in all theatres drove many of the advances in long-range naval gunnery that were later applied to the battle fleet. As one of now only two surviving warships of World War I, *M33* not only enjoys a particular national significance, but her singularly distinguished record of combat gained in one of the most dramatic campaigns of the war, which shaped forever the destinies of the ANZAC peoples, gives her a much wider significance. This is particularly the case if her important role in 1919 – where she provided naval gunfire support for European forces during the bloody civil war in North Russia (following the Bolshevik Revolution) and helped in their subsequent evacuation – is added to her service at Gallipoli. With all the associated meanings and complex geo-political, imperialist and cross-cultural connotations suggested by both these key events in the age of catastrophe which ushered in the 20th century, she has a legitimate claim to international significance.

ASSOCIATIONAL LINKS

The career of this modest little warship between 1915 and 1919, the significant period of her life and history, thus may be said to offer rich opportunities for both the interpretation of a distinctive aspect of the operational history of the Royal Navy in World War I, and more widely for the education and greater public understanding of the economic, social and geopolitical context within which the history and experience of citizens of the 20th Century was in large part shaped.

FORMAL OR AESTHETIC QUALITIES

Being merely a steel-built, steam-driven hull of simple form and construction specially designed with a shallow draft as a floating gun platform for a wartime purpose, *M33* cannot be said to embody any important technological innovation or other feature of distinctive nautical import. However, evidence does exist to suggest that the smaller 6-inch gun monitors began in embryo as a rough sketch drawn almost literally on the back of an envelope by the then Director of Naval Construction, Sir Eustace Tennyson d'Eyncourt, during a meeting with Sir Winston Churchill, First Lord of the Admiralty, and Admiral Sir Jacky Fisher, First Sea Lord, in March 1915. Furthermore, much of the basic design for the larger monitors had been carried out by Charles Lillicrap, who also seems to have taken over the design of the smaller vessels, and he too went on to become Director of Naval Construction (1944-1951), so her lineage is of interest.

5
THE CONSERVATION GATEWAY

5

Decision time

THE CONSERVATION GATEWAY

Analysing the importance of a vessel will enable a decision about the best conservation method to adopt in order to retain her significance. This book identifies this crucial point in an owner's journey as the Conservation Gateway, where a choice must be made about whether to conserve the vessel primarily for her fabric, or to keep her in operational use. Both options will have an impact on the conservation processes to be employed and involve losses of one kind or another.

Previous page: Once the vessel has been stabilised and thoroughly assessed, it is time to make a decision about which conservation route to adopt.

The working capacity of a vessel nominated for conservation of her fabric in static form will be removed by preservation for display. Inevitably, fabric will be destroyed when efforts are made to keep the vessel operational. Looking ahead through the gateway should alert owners to the conservation consequences of either route. One or other of these routes must be selected at this stage, as a half-way measure can result in a vessel's significance being lost by default. Whichever route is adopted, those involved must appreciate that there will be major cost implications that have to be met.

CONSERVATION OF FABRIC

In some cases, the fabric conservation route is obvious. *Mary Rose* is one of the best known examples of fabric conservation in the UK. She is displayed to the public ashore and under cover where the most intense and conscientious conservation techniques can be applied. Some 45% of her hull survives and almost nothing of her masts and spars, bar a fighting top, blocks and parrel balls. She could not be made fit to sail again with any of her original fabric intact. A sailing replica would not be the same ship and would have limited public access, so would only offer a solution if it could be built in addition to preserving the original fabric. As a result, there is a general consensus that *Mary Rose's* fabric as it is, resurrected from the seabed along with the stunning artefacts found inside her, is such a source of wonder and historical importance that its preservation in a controlled environment with public access is the right answer. However, the nature of old waterlogged wood as in vessels such as *Mary Rose* and *Vasa* is very different to the 'wet wood' encountered in the process of conserving 'surface' ships. The latter, whilst perhaps not in the best of condition, is far more structurally robust and malleable and is therefore open to a variety of processes and approaches.

Facing page: Vessels destined for static display in a controlled environment, as here at National Maritime Museum Cornwall, clearly demand the fabric conservation route.

5

THE CONSERVATION GATEWAY

5

There are less historically significant vessels, in better condition than *Mary Rose*, that also richly deserve the maximum preservation of their fabric, which almost always means static conservation undercover. For example, any surviving vessel from the 18th Century or before, even a modest rowing boat, is so rare that static conservation as near 'as found' as possible and in a protected environment is generally the preferred choice. The case for the static conservation of substantially complete or unique surviving examples of more recent types of working boat can be less obvious. Just as with vernacular buildings, we have often been slow to recognise the historical value of these rarities as part of the distinctive regional history of ordinary people.

The original fabric of vessels kept ashore and undercover can be conserved in the long term if they are kept in an environment with maximum protection. This might mean keeping the vessel indoors, or providing ingenious covers to prevent rain penetration and damage from ultra-violet light or rapid changes in temperature. Depending on the quality of the decisions made, the condition and complexity of her construction, and the skill of the people who undertake the work, it is possible to slow down and, in some cases, virtually halt deterioration. Large ships may have to be conserved in the open air, either afloat or in a dry dock if this can be found. Exposure to the elements, above and below the waterline, does not necessarily mean that their fabric will have to be replaced over time, but it does make preservation more challenging. Preservation of a large-scale vessel undercover is probably appropriate only for a very small number of ships of outstanding importance.

Historic vessels in museum ownership or large collections are not always the most representative or the best preserved examples of their type. Curators and trustees need to regularly review their collections and be aware of duplication in other museums or private ownership. They may have to make hard decisions about disposal or tactfully refuse gifts. They must be sure that limited budgets are being spent on effective conservation of the most significant craft and remind themselves of the conservation route chosen and whether this remains the most appropriate way forward. Equally important are a good quality care plan and a conservation strategy designed to retain a vessel's significance. Keeping vessels in store in stable conditions can be a useful interim measure for a museum or private owner, giving time to make good conservation decisions and raise funds for the work.

Ships and boats kept ashore or in a covered dry dock without special environmental controls may be protected from the weather and are significantly safer, but still need regular maintenance and a good understanding of the impact of their environment,

Facing page: The lifeboat collection at the Historic Dockyard, Chatham, is conserved for static display and kept under cover, thereby reducing the maintenance that would be required if the vessels were exposed to constant external weathering.

including visitors, on their fabric. Static vessels displayed in the open air, where they are vulnerable to rainwater, the effects of direct sunlight or subject to frosts will only survive for a finite period of time. There is little point in applying for grant aid for work on their fabric, because the results are likely to be short lived. A boat or ship kept on dry land is not in the medium for which her structure was designed. Ensuring internal structural integrity and adequate external support are important considerations but, in most cases, are less problematical than keeping rainwater out of a vessel in the open air.

The circumstances of some historic vessels mean that static conservation afloat may be the only option. This has the advantage of keeping a boat or ship structurally supported in water, but the drawback is the almost inevitable replacement and reconstruction of fabric at and below the waterline. If she is also kept in the open air, damage from rainwater, sunlight, wind and changes in temperature is likely and should be controlled as far as is possible. She will need not only regular inspection and maintenance, but regular haul-outs or dry docking and her hull will eventually need fabric replacement. The bigger the ship, the more expensive periodic haul-outs or dry docking will be. In 1994, the cost of unmooring and re-mooring *Warrior* was £30,000, before undertaking any of the essential work she needed. In 2004, the cost of unmooring and re-mooring had risen to £68,000 and the total cost of dry docking the ship was £454,000. A related problem for floating vessels held in static conservation is the difficulty of offering good public access to the lower hull while a vessel is displayed afloat.

For HMY *Britannia*, her purpose as a royal residence and her royal associations are more important to a wide audience than her operational use as a hospital ship. Her history is reflected in the exceptionally high standard of finish to her fabric, especially her coatings and fittings. She is now conserved at Leith, Edinburgh, where she can be enjoyed by visitors. The preservation of the original fixtures and fittings used by the royal family create a strong sense of authenticity that adds to this enjoyment.

This aspect of the public appeal of an historic vessel can be very important for her longer term viability and public profile, and should not be underestimated. Ships conserved primarily for their fabric are often likely to be in institutional or charitable ownership, with stated obligations to make use of the vessel in some way for the public good.

CONSERVATION FOR OPERATIONAL USE

Many owners are motivated to conserve historic vessels precisely because they wish to sail, steam or motor them, either for pleasure or in a commercial context. This keeps historic vessels alive, establishes a future for them (if not always the function for which they were designed) and brings pleasure, whilst developing the skills that come with operational use.

However, taking this conservation route will lead to the loss of original materials since the owner will be conserving function over fabric. Operating a vessel is incompatible with extensive preservation of original or surviving fabric and the principal conservation process applied will be replacement and reconstruction. The live link with the historic fabric of the past will be gradually eroded as rotten wood or rusting iron is replaced to maintain the seaworthiness and safety of the vessel, although this does not necessarily mean that the integrity of the vessel is lost. *Droleen II* is a 1948 Brittany Class yacht, designed by Laurent Giles and built by A H Moody for speed and adventure. She is not a unique survivor of her class and the elegance of her original design, particularly her high bow, is best appreciated when she is sailing. Returning her to operational use in the late 1990s restored her true design function.

Private owners of vessels often decide to return them to or conserve them for operational use, but might still feel that, ultimately, the vessel's significance will merit fabric preservation and public display. This is the 'sunset' approach to conservation for operational use, which recognises that a vessel which may be

THE CONSERVATION GATEWAY

Previous page: Small operational vessels like the ones seen here are often used for pleasure in private ownership. If a decision is taken that the vessel should continue to be used for this purpose, it will be important to maintain her well and accept that future reconstruction may be necessary.

Facing page: Victorian Royal Navy sloop HMS Gannet *has been in dry dock at The Historic Dockyard, Chatham, since 1987. She has been conserved as a static exhibit with adaptations to facilitate public access, such as the walkways on either side which can be seen in this image.*

fit to operate now, with a high percentage of original fabric intact, will reach a point where authentic fabric will have to be replaced unless she is retired before then and given a more protected environment. To be successful, the sunset approach needs very careful planning. It is important to identify which factors are likely to drive a decision to withdraw a vessel from operation, particularly those relating to the loss of original or surviving fabric and put her into a preservation regime. Whilst it is unlikely that the timing of this decision can be predicted, the conditions that will trigger it must be thought out.

OBSERVATIONS

Whichever conservation route is chosen, the vessel's fabric may still require adaptation. For vessels on static display, protection from the public will result in carefully designed walkways or barriers, which should be arranged so they do not interfere either with the ship or its preservation. If visitors come on board, further adaptations will be needed to accommodate them and fulfil responsibilities to make them safe and to allow maximum access, ideally without compromising the integrity of the design. Fire prevention and emergency egress are key concerns. If static ships are hired out for events, additional adaptations associated with serving food and providing licensed facilities may be needed, and these may be difficult to justify if they impact negatively upon the retention of a vessel's significance. Both HMS *Warrior* 1860 and HMY *Britannia* are good examples, where sympathetic adaptations have been made in order to allow visitors to access as much of the ship as possible.

The impact of operational use on the original fabric varies, depending on a vessel's condition and the type of use to which she is put. Private ownership simply requires a safe and seaworthy vessel, whilst a charter vessel will have more demands made on her to comply with regional safety requirements, SOLAS (Safety of Life at Sea), International Maritime Organisation (IMO) regulations and others. A chartered naval architect may need to be consulted in order to meet these regulations. These will be on a graduated scale, depending on the waters in which she is operated and the number of passengers she carries, and may require major adaptation of her historic arrangement as well as the provision of life-saving equipment to rigorous modern standards. It is important that the vessel owner investigates at an early stage exactly what adaptations will be needed for the conservation route chosen. This should be done before commencing any work to ensure that such works do not have major and irreversibly damaging effects on the vessel and that their design has the least impact on original fabric.

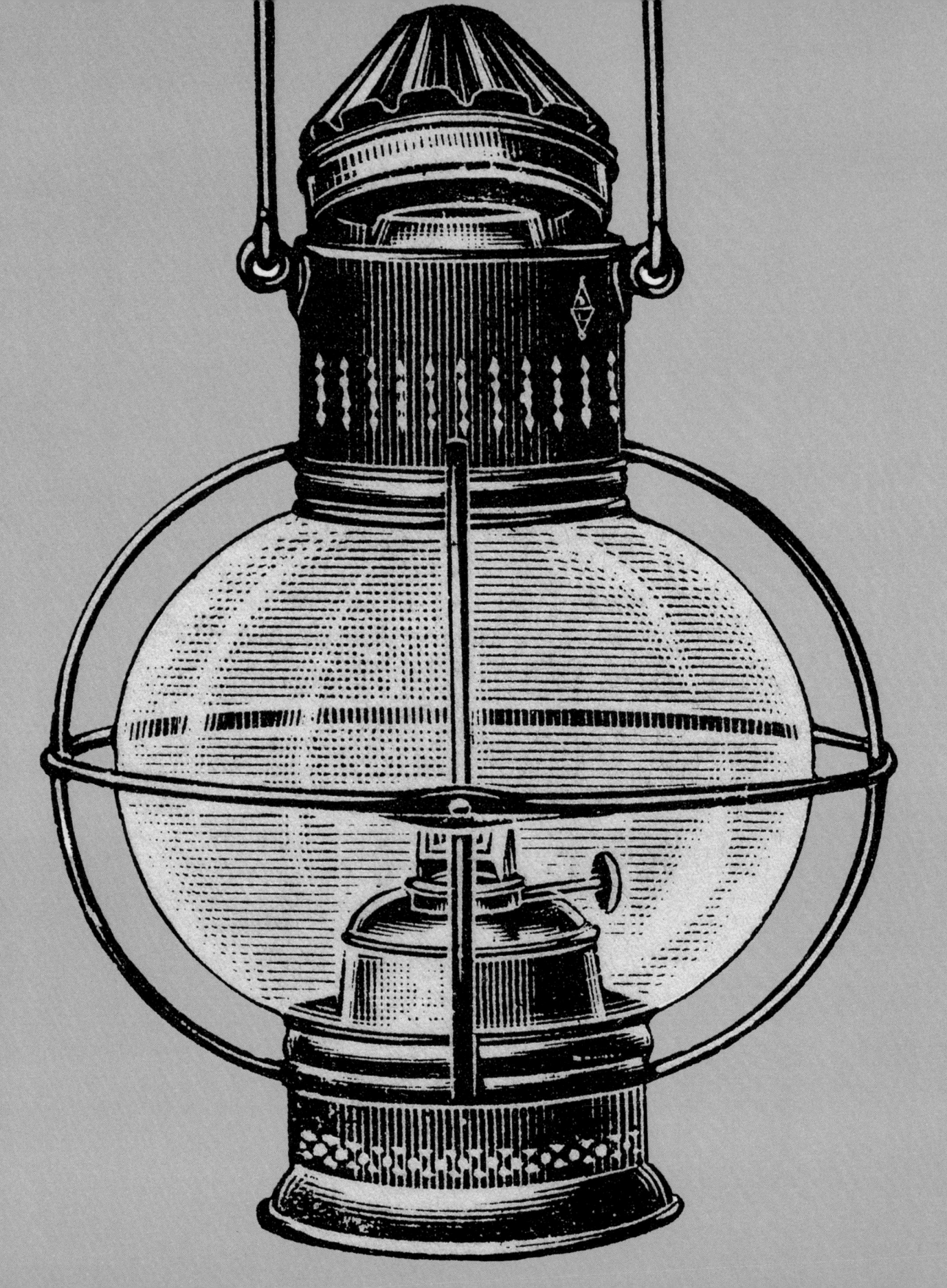

6

IDENTIFYING RISKS TO SIGNIFICANCE and ASSESSING PROJECT VIABILITY for the chosen conservation route

IDENTIFYING RISKS TO SIGNIFICANCE & ASSESSING PROJECT VIABILITY
FOR WHICHEVER CONSERVATION ROUTE IS CHOSEN

Identifying risks to significance determines the conservation management priorities of each project. Risks may relate to fabric, such as poor quality repairs in the past or conflicts of interest between the conservation needs of different materials. The human element can also present risks when owners find themselves unable to use or adequately maintain a boat.

Previous page: Paddle steamer Ryde *seen on the River Medina, delapidated and at risk of loss.*

Below: HMS Gannet *was built in 1878 from teak planking on a strong iron frame and powered by both sail and steam. She has now been conserved to her 1886 appearance, thanks to grant aid from the Heritage Lottery Fund and others.*

Volunteers who have not been properly trained, are badly supervised or may have a difference of view about what should be done can cause inadvertent damage. A change of direction in the management of a museum can put a boat collection at risk. The significance of the vessel must remain at the heart of all conservation activity and be properly understood. If this is put under threat it will impact on the outcome of the whole project. This chapter looks at how to analyse the potential dangers and ensure that a conservation scheme is viable.

As a first step, it is advisable to take the statement of significance or refer to it while noting down against each element of the vessel anything that represents a risk or a threat. These are not only direct problems affecting the vessel's fabric that might result from issues such as water penetration or rapid decay, which pressures a move into the restoration phase, but could also be indirect risks involving matters such as health and safety, the closure of a convenient dock for winter work or a fall in visitor numbers which may have an impact on funding for maintenance. For private owners, analysis of risk can be undertaken independently. However, with a formal conservation management plan produced for larger vessels, the person in overall charge of executive decisions should be actively involved, even when an outside consultant is preparing the plan. It is important that relevant members of staff or trustees are part of the consultation process when the plan is being written and, in certain circumstances, external agencies may equally have a part to play. At this early stage, it is vital that the views of all those with an interest in the vessel are captured, including the public. This is particularly relevant where the intention is to submit a funding application, since grant giving bodies like the Heritage Lottery Fund will expect to see evidence that this has been addressed in a supporting conservation management plan.

All owners will have a sense of what they want from their historic vessel, but may not have had enough time to think about the detail of how their set purpose could impact

on and perhaps damage the vessel. It is important to take enough time to consider this carefully. Charitable organisations will have stated legal and public benefit aims that will provide a context for decision making. Museums and similar organisations will have collections policies as well as national standards for the care of large objects and responsibilities to the public.

Legislation which applies to the vessel now or in the future may affect the success of a project. All owners will need to consider available resources, such as finances, skills, materials and time. This is not just for the immediate future, but for the long term, even after the project is completed. Starting work without careful planning may lead to major problems and delays later. Every case will be different, but as a starting point, the following key guidelines should be considered before any project is begun:

AVAILABILITY OF FUNDING FOR NECESSARY SHORT TERM WORKS

If grant aid is being sought, a business plan and a conservation management plan are likely to be required. These are also a good discipline for private owners.

AVAILABILITY OF MAINTENANCE AND LONG TERM CONSERVATION WORK SUPPORT

The right skills need to be sourced to carry out long term work on a vessel. These should include not only manual skills but, where applicable, those needed for overall project management, good governance of a trust, working with volunteers etc.

Facilities needed to conserve historic vessels are becoming increasingly difficult to find. This is Falmouth Dry Dock circa 1904, when docks like this were readily available. Today, SS Shieldhall, *one of the largest operational vessels on the National Historic Fleet, has to steam over 150 nautical miles from her home berth in Southampton to Falmouth, before she can find an affordable functioning dry dock able to accommodate her. Other surviving dry docks are at risk of loss: in Appledore, North Devon, Richmond Dock has fallen into disuse and is currently under threat from residential development.*

AVAILABILITY OF TIME AND ENERGY TO CARRY OUT BOTH RESEARCH AND PRACTICAL WORK

Proximity to facilities for hauling out or dry docking should be considered, as well as how secure these are likely to be. This is particularly important for vessels operated as static floating exhibits.

LEGISLATIVE REQUIREMENTS RESULTING FROM THE CONSERVATION ROUTE ADOPTED

The effect on the vessel's authenticity caused by compliance with MCA requirements and other legislative standards should be considered.

If a realistic assessment of the future costs of a project is to be achieved, a condition survey with cost indications will be essential. The condition of a vessel in operational use will have quite different requirements from a vessel destined for display ashore and undercover. Therefore, the brief for the condition survey should be clearly tailored to the chosen conservation route and the level at which the conservation process will be carried out.

The condition survey should be undertaken by a suitably experienced surveyor or shipwright who is knowledgeable and sympathetic to conservation. If the vessel is destined for preservation and display ashore then it may be appropriate to involve a skilled conservator. It is unlikely, nor intended, that a condition survey, especially for larger, complex vessels, will identify all detailed work that needs to be done. The purpose of the survey is not to create a work list for a yard, but to identify the key issues in the fabric that will need to be addressed in an appropriate manner according to the conservation route selected. The extent of rot or rust is often unclear until full work on the fabric is underway. A good working relationship and close co-operation with the boatyard or conservation workshop is essential to ensure that decisions on unexpected work are authorised only by the client and contained within a planned contingency allowance.

If after making an in-depth assessment of the vessel's significance and condition the project is demonstrably unviable, a decision may be taken to undertake preservation by record. Detailed information on recording and deconstructing historic vessels can be found in the first two volumes of this series, which are available online.[25]

Lifeboat George Elmy *is a significant part of Seaham's maritime history, having been involved in a tragic accident in 1962 during which five crew and four fishermen lost their lives. She is pictured here at risk, but has now been purchased for conservation as a living artifact to be enjoyed by school children and visitors.*

25 Kentley, Stephens & Heighton, *Understanding Historic Vessels* (2007)

IDENTIFYING RISK AND ASSESSING PROJECT VIABILITY
a quick guide

6

Assess thoughtfully what is putting the significance of the vessel at risk, both now and in the future.

Evaluate all external factors and how these will impact on the vessel's significance before deciding on a conservation route or starting work.

If an owner or organisation decides that the vessel cannot be conserved, make sure the following options are considered:

- stabilising her to buy more time whilst making decisions about her future
- passing her on to someone else who has the resources to conserve her
- recording her and archiving the details for public benefit before deconstruction, dismantling and perhaps safe storage.

It is essential to fully consider the long term management and maintenance costs and to include a contingency allowance for the project.

Recognise the value of a condition survey, but remember it is not a full list of all work to be done.

7

... beyond the conservation gateway

CONSERVATION PROCESSES

Whether a vessel is being conserved for operational use or static display will impact on the conservation process that is adopted. SS Robin *is seen here being lifted onto the purpose built pontoon on which she will be permanently displayed.*

7

Doing the work

CONSERVATION PROCESSES

What has been described in the previous chapters is a step-by-step approach to planning the conservation of any vessel.

The steps lead to two contrasting **Conservation Routes**:

Route A | Conserving a vessel principally for her **Fabric**

or

Route B | Conserving her principally in **Operational Use**

7

This book has provided a step-by-step approach to planning the conservation of any vessel. By assimilating and acting on this, the reader should have developed a thorough understanding of the vessel and consequently have made a clear decision about its future use. The next stage is to apply the appropriate conservation process or processes. The following four sections cover preservation, restoration, reconstruction and adaptation. These processes can be applied to all sorts of places, structures and objects, including vessels. Most conservation work on historic vessels, whether static or operational, will employ more than one process and some may use all four, but the balance between them should be determined by the chosen conservation route. Conservation for operational use naturally leads to a level of reconstruction, over time, to keep a vessel safe and seaworthy. The hull of a ship kept static afloat will also eventually need reconstruction, but it may be possible to preserve much of her interior. The full preservation of individual elements, such as fittings, can be combined with restoration, reconstruction and adaptation. However, preservation of a whole vessel requires keeping her static ashore and undercover and is most likely to be undertaken in a museum or other public context.

7.1 PRESERVATION

PRESERVATION

7.1

PRESERVATION MEANS KEEPING PART OR ALL OF A VESSEL'S FABRIC AS FAR AS POSSIBLE IN ITS EXISTING STATE & RETARDING DETERIORATION.

Preservation is the conservation process recommended for a vessel when her fabric is judged to be of such significance that as much of it as possible should be kept. She might be a masterpiece of innovative design; an acknowledged national treasure; significant for her great age, or the most complete surviving example of a once common type. Preservation provides a tangible bridge to the past, since the vessel is a material object which still survives today. This conservation technique produces an integrity that can only be maintained for any length of time by sacrificing operational use. Preservation may also be applied to significant discrete features and elements of static or operational vessels, in combination with other conservation processes. It is the recommended conservation process when research, observation and analysis have been unable to provide the evidence on which careful restoration or reconstruction could be based.

Preservation of fabric has wide potential value. It satisfies public demand for the 'real' thing. A preserved boat may be displayed in a museum and act as an authentic reference point for the conservation of operating vessels of the same type or vessels with features in common. It may be used to construct a true or operational replica. Original fabric is a library of information that is not held in any paper records and which may extend far beyond an understanding of past maritime craftsmanship and industries to an appreciation of places and events or the history of materials, their use in construction and later deterioration. In this way, preservation may help future generations answer questions that we have not yet thought of asking.

WHEN PRESERVATION SHOULD BE APPLIED

Preservation is usually applied to vessels that are accessible to the public, in a museum or similar, although vessels can also be preserved in store. Size is always a consideration as well as condition. A project to preserve a small open boat can be a major task, but the degree of difficulty and cost rises with larger and more complex vessels. *Vasa* is 180 ft long and sank while leaving Stockholm on her maiden voyage in 1628. Using a similar

Previous double page spread:
The National Museum of Ireland's workshop in Dublin where the Asgard *preservation project was carried out.*

Facing page:
The ss Great Britain *has now found a permanent and customised home in the very dock in which she was built.*

PRESERVATION

Facing page: The 18th Century French Admiral's barge, known as the Bantry Boat, *is seen here at various stages during the preservation work which led to her conservation for static display.*

approach to that which was later applied to *Mary Rose*, she was raised from the seabed and her waterlogged timber washed with chilled fresh water and then sprayed with polyethylene glycol. She was then slowly dried out and displayed in a climate-controlled building designed specifically both for her conservation and for public access. Although initially a great success, indications of sulphuric acid damage began to emerge some years after *Vasa* was placed on public display. Her conservation scientists are working to address this problem. Recovery of both these ships has been categorised by some as archaeology, but they also represent one end of the preservation process that has been applied to other large vessels.

Amongst the most rigorous preservation projects there are a small number of internationally significant vessels like these where the greatest care is taken to preserve their fabric by retarding decay and, where necessary, re-establishing or supporting structural integrity before displaying them in a controlled environment to slow down decay. These vessels deserve the same level of care that would be applied to any national treasure. Given the complexity and size of historic vessels, difficult decisions have to be made about the level of intervention needed to ensure longevity. These are likely to involve both engineers' and shipwrights' skills as well as the essential conservators. If a vessel is to be displayed to the public as she was at a particular time, preservation techniques may sometimes be combined with a measure of reconstruction.

Preserving a vessel's authenticity whilst retarding deterioration is no simple matter. Depending on condition and character, a wide range of techniques may be employed from delicate paint conservation and wood consolidation, to more robust intervention to retard rust and rot. The process of preservation for a boat or ship, particularly if it includes stripping coatings or targeted dismantling to correct problems, is akin to putting a magnifying glass to her fabric. Discoveries are inevitably made about the history of changes to her and new strands of research may need to be undertaken to try and explain what is found. Any whole vessel worth preserving deserves a publication to explain not only her significance but also the in-depth knowledge that is acquired when working on her. It is important to follow formal museum standards in labelling and storing any fabric removed, so that the biography of her fabric can be re-assembled.

At the other end of the preservation spectrum, small boats of varying degrees of significance may be kept undercover and ashore in stable environments that are not damaging to their materials. It is beneficial to segregate collections of boats, whether displayed or in store, according to their materials and provide the correct environmental controls, which will limit deterioration, for each group. If boats kept in store are not

7.1

PRESERVATION

An artist's impression of the Clovelly picarooner Little Mary, *now in storage at the National Maritime Museum Cornwall.*

neglected and in reasonable condition they are considered to be subject to 'preventive' or 'passive' conservation. They need little more than regular inspection and cleaning to remain stable, but may need major work in the future, depending on their significance. It can be a useful holding operation, and vessels which can be kept this way may benefit from future developments in conservation which address the particular needs of the vessel concerned. However, passive and preventive conservation must not be considered a 'hands-off' approach: it must be actively and carefully managed, based upon a thorough technical understanding of construction, fabric and intended environment.

Little Mary is a Clovelly herring fishing boat, known as a picarooner or 'sea robber', built circa 1898 in Appledore, Devon, and now part of the collection at the National Maritime Museum Cornwall. To put her back on the water would require almost complete reconstruction and lose the simple but telling signs of wear and repair in fabric that are largely original. For instance, there is a tingle (patch) which illustrates her vernacular character and is an 'honest mend', using a visible plaster of lead or copper and fitted over damage with minimal regard for appearance as would be expected for a working vessel. This repair is an important element of authentic fabric which should be preserved. *Little Mary* is currently kept in storage, undercover and ashore, with regular inspection and cleaning to check her condition. In this way, her original fabric is preserved and students on the Falmouth Marine School traditional boat-building course have used her hull as the model to build a replica for operational use.

7.1

Boats and ships kept in museums or similar environments are by no means all conserved by preservation and the operational use route may be chosen for them. This may be the result of considered judgement or an accident of history. A curator or manager may believe their level of significance is better served by keeping them afloat or in occasional use. Before the late 20th Century, vessels in museums, with the exception of very ancient small boats, which were identified as archaeology, were often hastily reconstructed to sailing condition or, with display in mind, reconstructed to give visitors a visual impression of pristine condition. The earlier the date at which an historic vessel ceased to operate and was conserved, the more likely she is to have been reconstructed rather than preserved. This has left an inheritance of nationally important vessels in the UK, such as HMS *Victory*, which have been extensively, and repeatedly, reconstructed.

Preserving a whole vessel, or most of it, is a recent approach to boats and ships of significance built in the 18th, 19th or 20th Centuries. The Merseyside Maritime Museum led the way in the 1980s and 90s. John Kearon, who became the Head of Shipkeeping, Industrial and Land Transport Conservation for National Museums, Liverpool, worked with a specialist team that was developed at the museum. They proved that strict conservation ethics and processes could be applied to vessels, even in poor condition, preserving a much higher percentage of original fabric than had previously been thought possible. Through this approach they also discovered far more than is usually understood of how the vessels had been adapted and changed in their lifetime. In the process of their involvement with several ferrous fastened wooden historic vessels, the interaction between wood and differing metals became of growing concern to the team.

This approach was also adopted with the 'Bantry Boat', a vessel of international importance because of her age. She is an 18th Century French admiral's barge owned by the National Museum of Ireland, and has been meticulously preserved in an exemplary manner for her significance, including all the evidence of damage and wear that testify to her age. She was first rigorously examined, photographed and recorded, and all surfaces were cleaned of dirt, grime and graffiti. Her coatings (paint analysis established that they were not original, but probably early-mid 19th Century) have been cleaned and consolidated as found. Mouldings on the after quarter backrests, formed in the classic French Navy lozenge shape, were cleaned and conserved, with missing sections replicated in original form in order to give the ornamentation the emphasis that its significance deserved. However, the new elements were left without coatings to distinguish them from the original fabric. The main structural problem proved to be that the centres of each of her sawn floors had rotted away and the keel had broken into four pieces with the aftermost portion missing. The preservation approach to this was to save, conserve and consolidate all original fabric wherever possible. Discoveries made during this process also led to a radical re-interpretation of her history from the archaeological evidence in her fabric. In her preserved state, she is over 90% original to at least 1796, the year of her capture in Bantry Bay.

PRESERVATION

PRESERVATION PROCEDURES

Facing page: The Swedish warship Vasa, *seen here in her purpose-built, air-conditioned Museum, following her extensive conservation programme during which she was sprayed with poly-ethylene glycol and then dried before being put on public display.*

Rot, rust and infestation that cannot be retarded by environmental controls should be treated using the least damaging and gentlest methods and only after recording any traces of coatings and wherever possible preserving samples for further research. Original fabric should be carefully protected when work is being undertaken to avoid inadvertent damage. The best available materials, products and methods for stabilisation or consolidation should be researched, including test panels, before extensive use. No irreversible modern techniques should be used without careful consideration. Reversible procedures should be adopted wherever possible in case more effective options are found in the future.

If a whole vessel is preserved ashore, adequate support must be provided for her at all times and her fabric stability and balance, which may be affected by drying out, monitored. An object file (a master document comprising all known information) and care plan should be developed for whole vessels preserved in museums, including a non-destructive maintenance and cleaning strategy. The environment in which a preserved vessel is kept should be appropriate to her materials of construction. This should include generous ventilation for all parts of a vessel during preservation work and after. The impact of the environment on the different materials of a vessel is complex. The best environment for the preservation of a wooden vessel may not be the ideal environment for the metal fastenings and fittings that hold the vessel together. This is particularly so where iron or steel are involved or if a mixture of different metals are in close proximity. Ferrous metal corrosion can continue indefinitely under certain circumstances, even in environments considered ideal for wooden vessels, especially if chloride contamination is present.

It is possible and desirable to flag up any interventions made as part of the preservation process by various means. Introduced fabric can be left without coatings to clearly distinguish between old and new. New or replacement materials, which may be covered by renewed coatings, can be identified by branding, stamping, affixing welded tabs or other permanent means including the date of installation. So long as a paper or electronic record is kept carefully, replacement fabric can be marked up on a drawing or identified in a written record. A daily record of work undertaken will provide a more accurate account of what has been done than recollection when the work is completed.

A vessel in operational use will need periodic reconstruction of parts of her fabric but wherever possible, historic fittings should be preserved and, if consistent with safety,

7.1

Conservation of the ss Great Britain's *iron hull presented a difficult problem – it was too fragile to be moved, but the dock she was in offered a damp environment and experts predicted corrosion could destroy the ship within a few years. A clever solution was found by encasing the ship below the waterline in a giant dehumidification chamber, made by covering the dry dock over with a glass roof. In this way, the hull is preserved and visitors can view the underneath of the ship as well as going on board.*

kept in use. If this is not an option, they should be retained on board *in situ* or, where this is not possible, safely stored. There is a danger of conflicts of interest between the vessel and its visitors which may need to be protected from one another. The presentation and interpretation of vessels kept ashore and undercover is a challenge at any time, but museums need to be especially alert to risks to fragile fabric from the innocent desire to touch or look inside, or the possibility of vandalism.

OBSERVATIONS

No individual case is quite like another, but successful preservation requires a coherent balance between many different skills, depending on the condition, type and materials of the vessel. A vessel in poor condition will need the skills of conservators but may also call for a shipwright or boat builder with special experience of, and sympathy for, the structure of a vessel that is not going to be returned to the water. For a preservation project, shipwrights or boat builders may need to work in conjunction with a structural engineer and a range of conservators who might include specialists in timber, metal and paint analysis and conservation. The analysis of materials and their deterioration may require consultancy from specialist academic departments. Examples include work by the Department of Archaeological Conservation at Cardiff University for metal corrosion and Portsmouth University's contribution to the conservation of *M33* and *Holland 1*. Past experience suggests that the best work is done when teams of skilled people can be brought together or developed in-house at museums, learning from each new project.

PRESERVATION
a quick guide

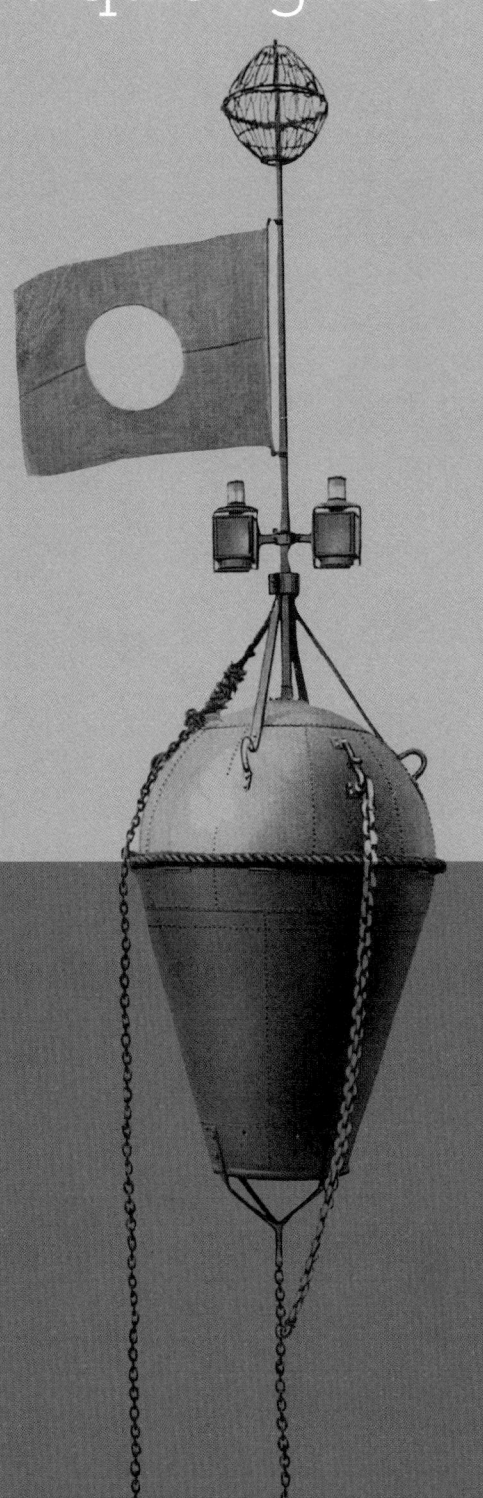

Significant elements of all historic vessels should be preserved unless there is a conflict with safety, or where preservation would jeopardise the vessel's future survival.

Long-term preservation of a whole vessel is usually only feasible if she is kept undercover and ashore.

Providing a controlled environment minimises the need for interventions into the fabric of a vessel. All interventions, including both fabric removal and new materials, should be recorded.

If deteriorated elements must be replaced, new elements should be distinguished from the original *in situ* wherever possible.

Remember not to confuse preservation with reconstruction or unnecessarily rob a vessel of her original fabric if she is destined for static display.

Make sure the importance of creating a stable, controlled environment as part of the campaign to retard decay is recognised.

Provide and regularly update interpretation for visitors to help them understand and enjoy the preserved vessel.

PRESERVATION CASE STUDY | ASGARD

ASGARD

Asgard, is a 51 ft (15.5m) wooden yacht, designed and built by Colin Archer in Norway in 1905. Today, she provides an excellent example of the technique of preservation. The National Museum of Ireland, following a decade of debate, made the decision to adopt the fabric preservation route and conserve her for static display, by saving her original materials as far as possible. This choice was fuelled by *Asgard's* significance in an Irish context through her famous gun-running voyage of 1914 when her owner, Erskine Childers, brought arms and ammunition into Ireland that were later used in the 1916 Easter Rising. Her iconic status, connection with Childers and significant pedigree as a Colin Archer-designed vessel all contributed to the outcome of preservation rather than reconstruction.

Asgard's original hull planking was fixed with brass boat nails and wooden treenails. In a salt-laden environment, the brass reacted with both original iron fittings and steel fastenings introduced later. Analysis by experts at Cardiff University found that both iron and steel fittings and fastenings were contaminated with chloride. This meant that corrosion would continue, even with the vessel out of the water and dry indoors. She was riddled with actively corroding fastenings, all of which had affected adjacent wood. Consequently, project manager John Kearon, Master Shipwright and Ship Conservator, led a small team of four craftsmen in removing all iron and steel fixtures and fittings in order to stabilise the vessel. Over two years, the vessel was effectively deconstructed in a co-ordinated process, to allow her structure to be analysed, consolidated and preserved wherever possible.

With the aim of conserving maximum hull structure, they used engineers' hole-saws to bore around each fastening to the thickness of the plank. This allowed each plank to be lifted off the nails, which could then be extracted separately. With all degraded wood removed, the holes were plugged, badly damaged areas given localised repairs and the planks put back into place, held in by new silicon bronze wood screws. With similar corrosion damage to the frames and deck-beams as well, this proved a time-consuming and exacting process. It quickly became clear that had the approach been for operational sail use, all planking and framing would have been lost: such was the extent of corrosion-induced damage throughout the vessel. This would have made *Asgard* a full reconstruction, or a replica, rather than surviving with the great majority of her original hull structure and deck intact and stable.

The project was supported by extensive research into the vessel's history, including use of archive correspondence incorporating Colin Archer's hand-written specification for *Asgard's* build. However as work continued, the vessel herself – in her structure, markings and different woods – offered inherent evidence of past alterations and additions. The team has recorded every aspect of the work, with a project diary and both still and moving images. When complete, *Asgard* will be displayed in her original form as built. John Kearon concluded that she will demonstrate the fundamental difference between using conservation techniques of preservation against those of reconstruction for further use; "one destroys in order to 'save', the other saves without destroying".

7.2 RESTORATION

7.2

RESTORATION

RESTORATION MEANS RETURNING THE EXISTING FABRIC OR PART OF THE FABRIC OF A VESSEL TO A KNOWN EARLIER STATE BY REMOVING ADDITIONS OR RE-ASSEMBLING EXISTING COMPONENTS WITH THE MINIMUM INTRODUCTION OF NEW MATERIAL.

Previous double page spread: Auxiliary schooner, De Wadden, *was the last merchant sailing ship to trade on the Mersey. She ceased trading in 1961.*

Restoration is the recommended conservation process for vessels, or their parts, when additions or changes are judged to obscure significant fabric and their removal is a benefit. For example, the removal of an added superstructure may better reveal the lines and arrangement of an earlier phase, but should only be undertaken if that phase is clearly more significant. Historic features that have been removed in the past may also be found, repaired and reinstated.

Most vessels of any age are the product of adaptation and change. Boats and ships were often altered for some reason during their working lives. Secondary and subsequent phases are not only part of their story but may have offered valuable improvements or be rare and interesting. The removal of elements to reveal earlier features or to replace with those which reflect a specific phase in the vessel's history needs to be justified to ensure that the vessel is not being robbed of an important part of her autobiography. Minimal new fabric should be introduced in any restoration and care must be taken to ensure that guesswork or preconceived notions do not lead to replication. Items removed from the vessel should be recorded and then stored or disposed of according to their significance.

Facing page: The restoration of De Wadden *is being undertaken by the Shipkeeping & Land Transport Conservation Department at the Merseyside Maritime Museum.*

When making the decision about restoring a vessel to a certain time in her life, it is important to make sure there is a compelling reason for doing this, rather than conserving her 'as is' with all the phases of her autobiography intact. The owner should assess why the chosen period is more important than any other, using the understanding achieved through research, and investigate how much fabric survives from that era. The amount of fabric which will have to be removed in order to restore the vessel to the relevant year should be considered, as well as the work needed to make good the materials which are revealed. It will be necessary to carry out further off-ship research about the timeframe to which the vessel will be returned, using existing examples, photographs, drawings, descriptions and other sources so that the

7.2

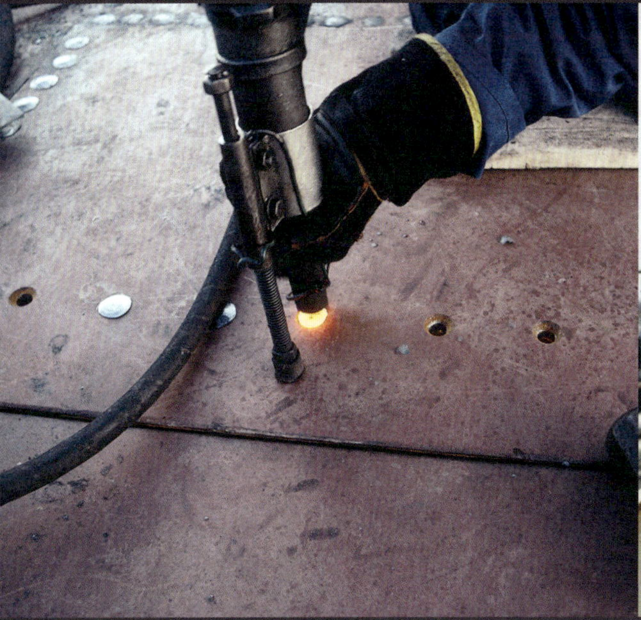

Implacable *was a 74-gun ship, built as the French* Duguay-Trouin *at Rochefort in 1800. She fought at the 1805 Battle of Trafalgar on the French side, but was captured about a month later and taken into the Royal Navy. She was scuttled in 1947 and her figurehead and stern carvings were given to the National Maritime Museum, Greenwich. Her stern carvings consist of 56 separate parts, which can be seen here restored for display and reassembled on a replica transom.*

restoration can be carried out thoroughly, without conjecture. Before starting, the owner should check that the appropriate materials, fittings and finishes can still be obtained. Features of the vessel which are to be removed should be recorded whilst they are still in place. For vessels where fabric is the priority, special skills for making good may be needed and great care should be taken to avoid damage when elements are removed.

An example of these issues is the deck house of *De Wadden*, a Dutch-built, steel auxiliary schooner of 1917, now under a 'slow burn' restoration programme at the Merseyside Maritime Museum. Photographic and physical evidence showed that, at some time in the 1960s, the riveted steel main hatch coamings had been extended upwards and roofed over to become a deck house, using poor quality and inappropriate steel plating. This was done during her phase as a sand dredger and was judged, after due consideration, to be less significant than her primary Irish Sea trading role. Therefore, the raising of the coamings was reversed as part of the conservation project undertaken by the Ship-Keeping Department.

RESTORATION
a quick guide

7.2

Understand what is meant by the term 'restoration' as used in this publication.

Make sure the value of secondary and later phases are not underestimated and removed unnecessarily.

Carefully consider the extent and nature of new work needed to make good after removal of fabric.

RESTORATION CASE STUDY | OTTO

7.2

OTTO

In Spring 2007, the Lakeland Arts Trust acquired with the help of the National Heritage Memorial Fund (NHMF) the significant collection of steam boats and other craft assembled in Windermere by George Pattinson, which was offered to the nation by his family after he died. This legacy comprises craft at all levels of conservation and the Trust's staff have been working with National Historic Ships to apply the principles set out in *Conserving Historic Vessels* across the whole collection.

Otto was built in 1896 by Forrest & Son of Wivenhoe and is a magnificent example of the private steam yachts designed for pleasure at the turn of the 20th Century. She has a riveted steel hull, a triple expansion engine made by Sisson & Co. of Gloucester and canopied open accommodation for some 10 to 12 guests out for a party on the lake. National Historic Ships and other advisors to NHMF evaluated this vessel and confirmed that she is of national significance and should be acquired as part of the overall collection. Subsequently, the Lakeland Arts Trust undertook a review of the whole collection, identifying potential risks to significance and assessing project viability for each vessel in order to decide which conservation route should be adopted and the most appropriate conservation process to follow within that route.

Further analysis of *Otto* confirmed that she is in very good general order, with a minimal need for replacement of structure, equipment or fittings. The overall condition of the vessel, and her relationship to the other vessels in the collection helped the Trust make the decision to conserve her by restoration, with the capability for operational use. However, operating her will be limited to demonstrations due to certain features of the original design which make her difficult to steer: the rudder is positioned forward of the propeller making her hard to control at low speeds and therefore not suitable for regular passenger trips.

Trust staff have drawn up an outline project plan which will be refined ahead of the restoration programme being implemented. Detailed surveys indicated that between 5% and 10% of the riveted plating will need to be replaced like for like, with some concentrated work at the stern where there has been greater deterioration. The hull will then be carefully cleaned and repainted. The rudder, propeller, drive shaft and stern glands will all have to be removed, cleaned, repaired as necessary, and then re-positioned. The engine housing must be removed to allow the engine to be lifted out, stripped down, rebuilt and put back, whilst the boiler will also have to be removed, re-tubed and repositioned. Once the mechanical work has been completed, the engine housing and other deck fittings will be put back, cleaned or sanded as appropriate, and then repainted or revarnished. When finished, *Otto* will have been restored to her 1896 condition and configuration with minimal introduction of new material.

7.3

RECONSTRUCTION

73

140

7.3

RECONSTRUCTION MEANS RETURNING ALL OF THE FABRIC OR PART OF THE FABRIC OF A VESSEL TO A KNOWN EARLIER STATE BUT IS DISTINGUISHED FROM RESTORATION BY THE INTRODUCTION OF SIGNIFICANT NEW MATERIAL INTO THE FABRIC

Reconstruction is the most commonplace conservation process applied to the structure of boats and ships that are operational. It is often used to conserve their operational function by making the structure of the vessel safe. This involves replacing fabric that has deteriorated with new material. If this work is undertaken as a conservation process, the physical integrity of the vessel can be retained by being faithful to the materials, form, fastenings and coatings. These should be replaced like-for-like wherever possible in order to achieve the chosen phase in the life of the vessel. This is not the same as traditional 'repair', which might not repeat the past in this meticulous way. Reconstruction also differs from maintenance, described later in this book, which deals with the daily tasks needed to keep a vessel in good order.

Reconstruction is frequently applied to vessels or their parts, whether operational, static or displayed in a museum context, to re-establish significance. This can be done by recreating, on the basis of careful research, elements that have been lost or are so damaged that they cannot sensibly be preserved. However, without careful research and enough information on which to base reconstruction, there is a risk of making up a past that never existed. A record of what has been reconstructed, why, and how it was done should be made and passed on to future managers or owners so that the way the fabric of a boat has evolved and changed is clear. There are historic vessels where the failure to record reconstruction means that later owners are unable to identify what is original fabric and what is not.

Reconstruction as a conservation process is not the same as simply making an old vessel fit to move on water. Captain Joshua Slocum sailed round the world between 1895 and 1898 in the *Spray*, a 36 foot (10.97 metres) sloop, which he rebuilt for the purpose. He wrote: 'Now it is a law in Lloyd's that the *Jane* repaired all out of the old until she is entirely new is still the *Jane*. The *Spray* changed her being so gradually that it was hard to say at which point the old died or the new took birth, and it was no matter'. [26]

Previous double page spread: Spry *is a Severn trow, built in 1893 to carry cargo around the Bristol Channel and West Coast. After she retired, she languished as a hulk for some 25 years before being rescued. She has now been reconstructed and is on display at Blists Hill, part of the Ironbridge Gorge Museum.*

Facing page: Lifeboat Aguila Wren *was built in 1951 and part-funded as a memorial to Wrens lost in the torpedoing of SS* Aguila *in 1941. She is now being conserved to her original specification as an active memorial to those lost during the Second World War. Conservation of the vessel has involved a mix of two processes: restoration and reconstruction. Wherever possible, existing fabric has been retained but, as a bespoke vessel, some replacement parts such as the tabernacle have had to be specially manufactured to a Royal National Lifeboat Institution pattern.*

26. Slocum, Capt. Joshua, *Sailing Alone Around The World* (Adlard Coles Nautical: London, 2006)

RECONSTRUCTION

Facing page: Daystar *was built in 1894 by Crossfields of Arneside in Cumbria and is a sail fishing boat, known as a 'Nobby' or Morecambe Bay prawner. She is seen here undergoing a conservation process that involved both preservation and reconstruction practices to save as much original material as possible and return her to her original built form.* Daystar *is now in store at the Merseyside Maritime Museum.*

This is sometimes quoted as a light-hearted defence of what often happens when an old boat is made fit for re-use. This can be the creation of an entirely new boat or ship, not only in materials, but with significant changes to her design, or even her size. Slocum had not the slightest interest in conserving the old *Spray*, as the detailed description of his work demonstrates, but was building a new boat, apparently on the lines of the old, but customised to his needs, arranged and fit for an epic journey '...as strong as wood and iron could make her' and rebuilt '...timber by timber and plank by plank', with a different sheer from the old *Spray* and arranged specifically to hold the stores and include the kind of cabin he needed for a circumnavigation.

However, unlike the approach adopted by Slocum, in conservation terms the point at which 'the old dies and the new is born', does matter. It exchanges the traditional working use of a vessel with a purpose that puts significance first, rather than function. In practice, reconstruction is the broadest church of all the conservation processes. It can range from the recreation of a historic arrangement to major rebuilding for operational use. A vessel in poor condition can be reconstructed so she can be operated, using the original ship as a template and incorporating very little original fabric, perhaps no more than a transom and fittings. This is a form of recognised conservation, so long as it is undertaken with proper respect for, and repetition of, the evidence of the form, arrangement, materials, coatings and method of propulsion of the historic vessel and is accompanied by a record of what has been reconstructed and any departures from the template. Reconstruction that makes changes to form, arrangement or materials without justification referenced to significance is not conservation. There is a common pitfall here in that sometimes work is undertaken, but the vessel is not put back into operation at the end. This outcome will lose authentic original fabric without gaining any of the benefits of operational use.

Well conserved operational ships and boats tend, over time, to evolve into vessels with fabric from many different dates, all of which can be faithful to the vessel's integrity. There is a nice distinction between this evolution and beginning from scratch to build a replica. All conservation processes involve careful and considered judgement, but none more than reconstruction. It may be difficult to find like-for-like materials or trace skills that are fast becoming redundant in modern boat and ship building. Today's technology may have to be adapted to achieve the same results as those from earlier periods. For operational use there may be very good reasons for preferring modern fastenings to old, and many decisions about changes, small and large, will have to be justified and made. For example, making the choice to re-establish hemp rope and a bamboo mast on a Thames half-rater could prove a time-consuming and costly chase after materials,

7.3

RECONSTRUCTION

It can be difficult to source like-for-like materials when undertaking reconstruction work. In particular, owners experience problems locating timber and often have to find suitable wood from abroad if there is none available in the UK.

which will then be expensive to maintain compared with readily obtainable modern materials with a longer lifespan. However, owners dedicated to conservation believe that traditional materials and techniques are the best way to maintain authenticity and an understanding of the nature of the vessel. Those willing and able to undertake this level of conservation create a market for materials and skills, preventing them from disappearing.

Grant-giving bodies offering funding for conservation will expect owners to strive to achieve the highest quality workmanship and use of like-for-like replacement materials wherever possible. However, with the best intentions, the costs involved and the through-life maintenance of materials may militate against such an approach. Any compromises must be carefully justified. For example, the inclusion of an engine into a formerly unpowered craft is a common operational safety feature and conservation must be balanced against the practicalities of using a sail powered vessel today. It is important that owners adopting this approach think carefully about how to incorporate the engine and power train without compromising the vessel's integrity or spoiling her appearance and operational characteristics.

RECONSTRUCTION AS REPAIR TO MEET OPERATIONAL REQUIREMENTS

For operational vessels and those kept afloat, compliance with the requirements of external authorities, such as the Maritime and Coastguard Agency (MCA), will define the level of the work that must be done, but not its character. The right solution for maintaining significance should be carefully planned out in advance, including research on the availability of materials and skills that may be needed to ensure that the work is like-for-like. Owners should also recognise the possibility that MCA rules will not allow an accurate reconstruction.

When considering what needs to be done to meet modern operational standards, it is important to recognise that the MCA is open to discussion on how their requirements might best be met with minimum impact on the structure and appearance of the particular historic vessel. For vessels kept under cover, the attempt to reconstruct is likely to bring more difficult choices. If fabric is of significance and affected by rot and rust, external or internal splinting, propping and supports are more appropriate than replacing deteriorated or missing fabric. These can often be inserted very creatively without compromising the appearance of the vessel.

RECONSTRUCTION AS INTERPRETATION

Reconstruction may be part of the presentation and interpretation of an historic vessel. Communication with the public is essential for historic boats and ships in a museum or similar environment. If elements of a vessel are reconstructed to bring her 'alive' to the public, the work should be reversible and authentic materials need not be used, so long as the result looks, feels and even smells right. With this approach, it is important for the interpretation to show when materials significantly different to the original (such as modern plastics as opposed to wood) have been used. The Brunel engines of the ss *Great Britain* have been reconstructed so that visitors have an idea of the scale and impact of the technological achievement of her first phase. Lighter weight materials and careful prediction of the loads involved in making the engine turn (loads from which are carried down to the dock floor) help to ensure that the interpretation does not impact on the authentic fabric of the preserved ship. Equally, her six modern replica masts look and feel correct for 1845 but are in fact constructed from modern materials and carefully designed to give low maintenance, improved longevity and safety while appearing authentic. Where such approaches are adopted, it is important that those witnessing the results have some way of distinguishing what is real from what is reconstruction.

The Victorian yacht *Fricka*, designed and built by William Fife in 1894 was conserved by a blend of preservation and reconstruction in 2000. She was destined for display in the National Maritime Museum Cornwall and her owners wanted her returned to original built form for interpretation purposes, whilst retaining all existing original fabric. Detailed examination of the hull found that the sheers had been raised and her deck, beams and cockpit had been removed and replaced with an altered layout, probably some time in the 1930s. Both the stem and transom were in very poor condition and, once all non-original material had been removed, only the bare hull below the sheer level remained. The missing components, including sheer planks, deck beams, deck and cockpit carlings, and coamings, were all reconstructed using the same species of wood in original designed and built form. *Fricka* is now rigged and on museum display in Falmouth.

Gentleman's yacht, Fricka *is seen here on display in the National Maritime Museum Cornwall fully conserved. She was commissioned by Robert Mann, a prominent Glasgow businessman, and achieved seven first and eight second prizes out of twenty five starts in her first racing season.*

RECORDING CHANGES

It may be possible to identify reconstructed elements *in situ*. Depending on how an historic vessel is presented and interpreted, it is an honest approach to identify new fabric. Where there is no need to disguise it, for example, it is not concealed by a reconstructed coating, new structure should be distinguished from old by finish and should not be distressed to match the old. When new fabric is destined to be re-covered, it should be marked by stamping or other means, so that it can be identified if the coatings are replaced. Reconstructed detail can be distinguished from old by subtle changes, perhaps of moulding detail, which allow the whole to be 'read' as complete without disguising the distinction between new and old if looked at closely.

DOCUMENTING RECONSTRUCTION

Reconstruction can be documented by photography, measured drawings or sketches, supplemented by a written record. A daily log of work done is a reliable method of recording reconstruction as well as being useful in assessing time and costs of future work. The record should be archived and passed on with the vessel. A table identifying any alterations associated with reconstruction and the justification for change can provide a clear summary for future owners.

OBSERVATIONS

Many boat owners undertake reconstruction themselves, learning by their mistakes and from the advice of fellow enthusiasts. For larger vessels it is important to use a boat builder or shipwright with suitable experience, who is sympathetic to conservation and applies the principles in this book. The right naval architect will provide specification and mediate between the client and a shipyard and, where necessary, the MCA. Sight of past work and discussion with previous clients is a good way of choosing the appropriate people for the work. Commercial boat and shipyards without conservation experience often assess work on the basis of how quickly it can be done and may encourage an owner to use non-matching materials because they are to hand or familiar. A good working relationship between the client and whoever is undertaking reconstruction work is crucial. The level of new fabric required is unlikely to be clear until work is in progress and condition thoroughly understood. There needs to be an understanding that unexpected problems will turn up but that solutions require authorisation from the client and there may be delays while alternatives are considered. Clear planning and anticipating problems are essential to ensure the owner retains direction and control of the project.

RECONSTRUCTION
a quick guide

7.3

Reconstruction in the form of periodic renewal of fabric is inevitable for *operational* vessels in order to keep them safe and seaworthy.

Reconstruction is appropriate only where an historic vessel is incomplete through damage, alteration or deterioration and only where there is enough evidence to reproduce an earlier state of the fabric.

Traditional techniques and materials are preferred in reconstruction and any departure from this needs to be carefully justified.

If not in excessive conflict with the visual integrity of the vessel, reconstructed elements should be identifiable *in situ*.

Reconstruction should be recorded and the record passed on to successive owners/managers.

RECONSTRUCTION CASE STUDY | CAMBRIA

CAMBRIA

Cambria is a 91 foot (27.73 metres) long Thames sailing barge, built in 1906 to trade between the east coast ports and the near Continent carrying varied cargoes such as coal, cement, grain and cattle feeds. She made her last commercial voyage in 1970 and, after falling into neglect, was taken over by a group of enthusiasts who formed the Cambria Trust in 1996. *Cambria* was stabilised and placed into a floating dry dock at Sittingbourne. In 2007, after years of careful planning, the Trust was awarded a grant of £990,000 by the Heritage Lottery Fund and moved to Faversham. *Cambria* was then covered over by a design based on Kent polytunnels and a steel walkway was built around her to facilitate access during the reconstruction.

Although early estimates indicated that at least 90% of the barge timbers would have to be replaced, master shipwright Tim Goldsack and his small team aimed to reconstruct the vessel for operational use within three years. Initially, large sections of the deck were removed to expose the original interior of the barge. The steel keelson was found to be severely corroded at each end and could not be saved. However, the original keel and floor were in excellent condition and formed the solid base from which reconstruction could commence. New oak floors and side frames were fitted and the stem and stern post lifted to return the full sheer to the barge. The old after deadwood was totally removed and replaced with a new timber 20 foot long. The forward deadwood was similarly replaced. Many new curved oak sections had to be fabricated in sections and these were shaped using plywood templates drawn from the inner lines of the main hull planking.

Once the inner skeletal framework of the barge was complete, work began to extend the inner wales and fit the first sections of outer planking. Each length of timber was skilfully measured and cut to size, then steamed using a 'boil in the bag' method for one hour per inch of timber thickness. Once ripe, the plank was slowly clamped into the shape formed by the frames and fastened into position with galvanised spikes. The process was then repeated for the second layer of planking. Joints were staggered and the two layers sealed with a felt, hot tar and horse manure mix. All timber was sustainably sourced, with much of the new oak taken from a private forest in Somerset.

A written diary and photographic record of the project was maintained by the Trust, outlining each stage of the work for the benefit of future owners and also indicating where changes had to be made to the vessel's original form. Much original memorabilia relating to the barge was sourced and the vessel was visited by descendants of the last skipper, Bob Roberts and the builder William Everard. Documents including the complete cargo log books from 1936-1970 helped the team understand the history of the vessel they were working on. The project also facilitated the re-growth of traditional maritime skills, with a two year shipwright apprenticeship scheme developed in partnership with local colleges. Once reconstruction is complete, *Cambria* is intended to be used for educational activities. The reconstruction remains faithful in not fitting an engine, so she will sail the south east coast as she always did – a 'carbon free' example of transport.

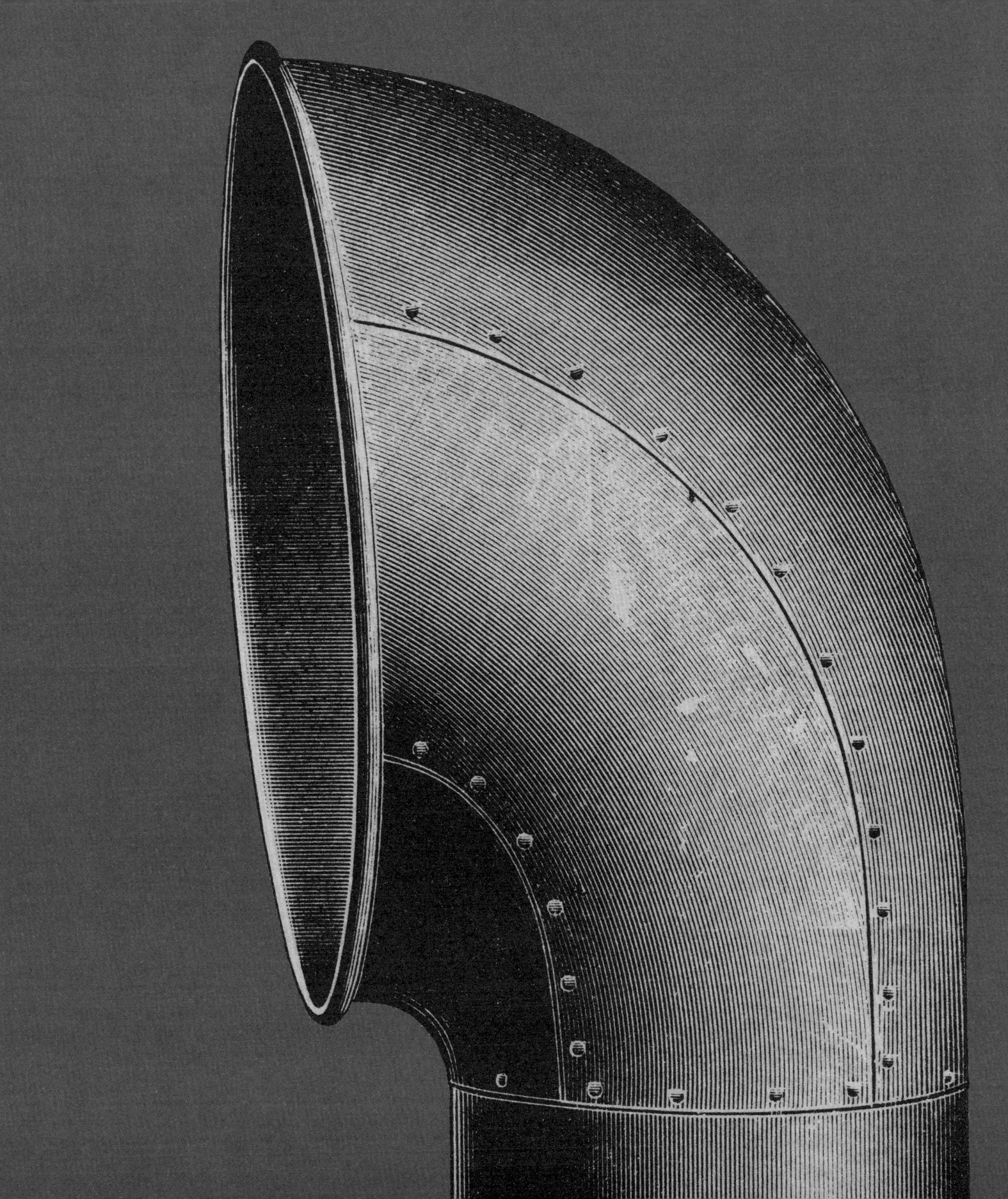

7.4

ADAPTATION

7.4

ADAPTATION

ADAPTATION MEANS MODIFYING A VESSEL TO SUIT A PROPOSED NEW USE

Previous double page spread: Waverley is operated by the Paddle Steamer Preservation Society and has been conserved to the style of her original build with well-disguised adaptations, necessary to meet current legislation.

A justified adaptation can bring benefits to a vessel if a modest loss of historic integrity leads to major gain in longevity. The most obvious examples of this are amendments to vessels in operational use, required by the Maritime and Coastguard Agency (MCA) on structural grounds before a vessel can operate legally. Adaptations to comply with health and safety and fire prevention may also be mandatory, whether a vessel is stationary or moves. There is much more choice for an owner in matters of security and the question of how much access can be sensitively managed for disabled visitors and staff on a static or moving vessel. The design of any adaptation should be carefully thought out to ensure the maximum benefit is achieved from the alteration and a minimal loss of fabric. An adaptation whose impact on the vessel's significance has not been fully considered can erode what is historically valuable about a vessel. Careful judgement needs to be made to avoid 'adaptation' being an excuse to make convenient or cost-saving changes, or solely to make operating the vessel easier. Some adaptations to historic fishing smacks to render them more efficient for racing, for example, are now being actively discouraged by a number of specialist groups, to avoid the loss of authentic character. Adaptations should be undertaken on the general principle that they can be reversed. This chapter looks at the occasions when an adaptation to fabric might be deemed necessary and the thought process applicable in each situation.

ADAPTATION TO COMPLY WITH STRUCTURAL INTEGRITY AND SAFETY

Facing page: HMS Cavalier, built in 1944 for the Royal Navy, was the last operational Second World War destroyer. She is seen here on display at the Historic Dockyard Chatham where a large number of visitors go on board each year.

Safety requirements for commercially operated or chartered vessels take precedence over original fabric. For a private owner running a vessel for personal use, safety is a matter of judgement and insurance. Replacing an unreliable historic engine with a newer model or adding an engine to a sailing vessel that never had one is about balancing risk against changes to significance. If the historic engine is not of significance and the risk to the safety of people and the vessel is high, replacement can make sense, although there may be other ways to keep the original in place. For vessels where the MCA has a legal responsibility, for example vessels over a certain size, or those carrying passengers, there will be external standards for structural integrity and safety. Ingenuity and care in applying the standards can minimise the level of adaptation required. It can be possible to keep redundant elements or introduce necessary changes such as modern lifesaving equipment and machinery by disguising them. It may make sense

7.4

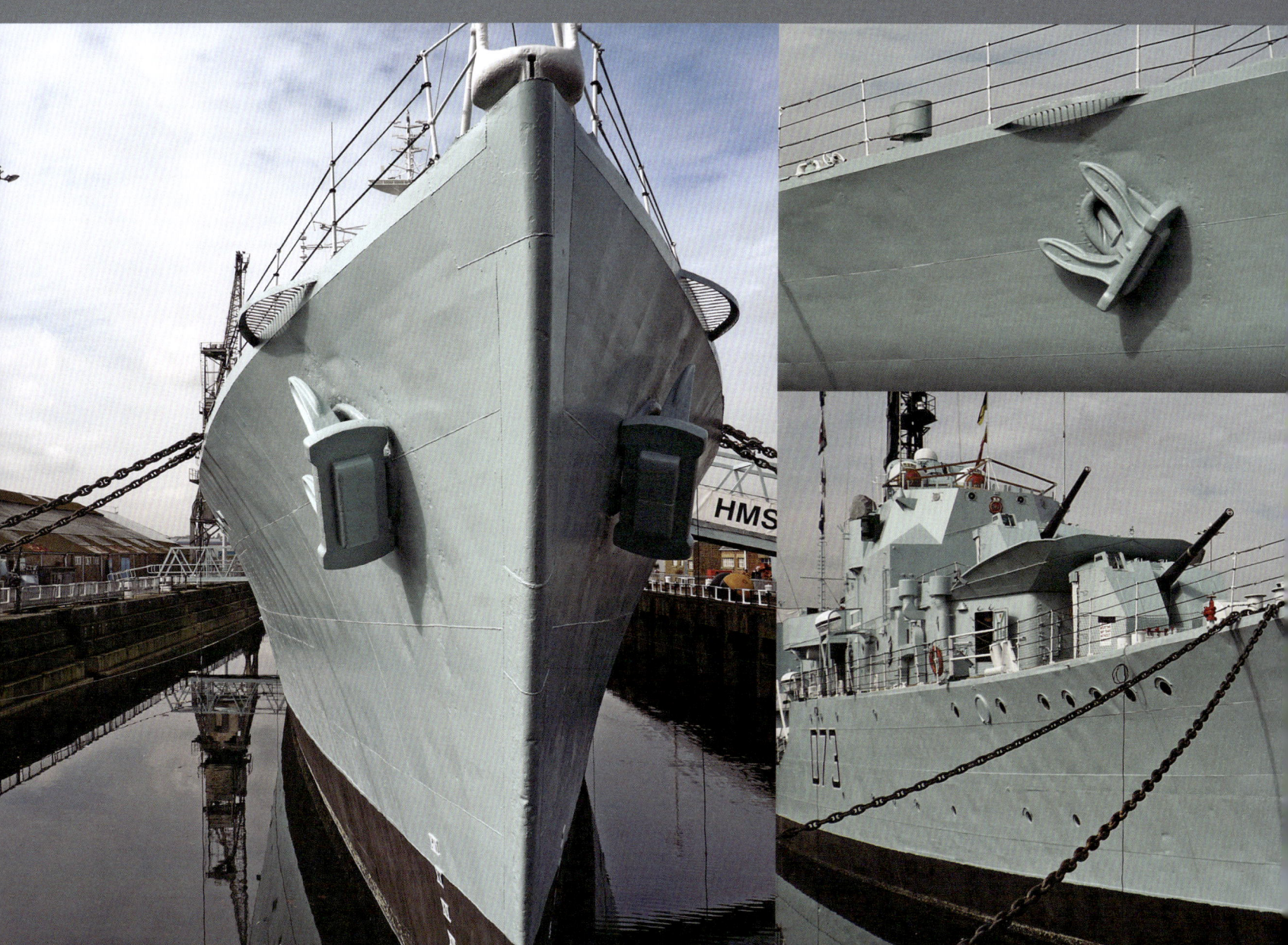

ADAPTATION

Reaper attends a regular programme of events during the sailing season. In 2009, she sailed more than 2000 miles, opened to the public on a total of 30 days at 19 events and welcomed over 17,000 visitors on board. She is a good example of an operational exhibit with very few adaptations.

to identify a specific and discrete 'non heritage' space in the ship's arrangement where these objects can be concentrated in order to avoid spreading modern adaptations throughout the vessel. The design of adaptations to comply with external regulations requires working with officials of the appropriate authority. It is useful to be able to cite known examples of adaptations on other vessels that have proved acceptable or represent clever solutions to problems.

Ingenious methods of adaptation were employed during the conservation of the paddle steamer SS *Waverley* for operational use, in order to comply with the MCA standards in relation to stability. The after-deck shelter was reconstructed in aluminium, not the original riveted steel in order to lighten the ship. In addition, one of *Waverley's* twin funnels had been previously replaced to a different design. Both funnels were reconstructed in aluminium fixed with bolts which met the twin purpose of re-instating the funnel's original appearance as a key element of the ship's profile and also lightening the ship, thus improving her stability. In addition, health and safety requirements saw the introduction of a hydraulic power pack for working the davits. The historic system of launching the lifeboats was by hand, but in order to be acceptable the new system had to be power-operated using hydraulic jacks. These were disguised to look like old ones with wooden blocks and ropes hiding the steel blocks. Modern buoyancy apparatus in the form of Mashford floats was also disguised in *Waverley's* seating.

ADAPTATION TO COMPLY WITH LEGISLATION IF VISITORS ARE INVITED ON BOARD

Health, safety and access for visitors on board may require adaptation. This is a delicate area. Disabled access can prove difficult to introduce to all parts of a ship given narrow through routes and vertical access to different decks and/or the dock. The ss *Great Britain* has a simple wheelchair lift system inserted into its funnel void without cutting or damaging any original fabric. HMS *Cavalier* has balanced the needs of visitors using the heads on board with historical accuracy by removing the doorway thresholds (originally there to reduce the danger of flooding) on some but retaining them on others, supported by suitable interpretation. However, the UK Disability Discrimination Act does not require access routes to be cut through original fabric. Instead reasonable alternate means of accessing or viewing spaces can be offered. In this context, HMS *Victory* has been required to construct an external tower alongside the ship to provide a suitable means of escape.

7.4

ADAPTATION FOR INTERPRETATION AND PRESENTATION

The motive to interpret and explain a vessel thoroughly to visitors may encourage adaptations to her fabric. Any owner of a publicly accessible vessel has responsibilities to visitors as well as objects in their care and these must be carefully balanced. As large functional objects, boats and ships can be difficult to display in static form. It can be a challenge to arrange for a visitor to see the whole shape of a vessel, both above and below the waterline, as well as being able to view the full superstructure or inside the hull of undecked vessels. A generous space for display and imaginative design, with ramps allowing for different viewing positions and use of glass waterlines or similar, can provide good visual access to a vessel without impacting on her fabric. Interventions to the fabric of a vessel for improved visual or physical access need to be considered not only against damage to significance, but also in the light of what technology may offer in the near future and the need to update interpretation regularly. Particular care should be taken when considering cutting new openings in bulkheads or cabin walls. Cutting sections from the hull to facilitate visitor access should be resisted in most cases, as this is likely to contradict the essential nature of her design.

Left: Access to the various parts of ss Great Britain has been cleverly integrated resulting in minimal disturbance to the original fabric.

Right: The wheelchair lift system hidden within the funnel of the ship.

ADAPTATIONS TO IMPROVE ACCESS FOR INSPECTION AND MAINTENANCE

Maintenance can be bedevilled by poor ventilation, and will require a certain level of access so inspection and remedial works can be carried out. If problems with a vessel's condition cannot be identified at an early stage and remedied, they may evolve into expensive and damaging replacement of fabric. Sensitively designed adaptations to improve ventilation, such as locks that allow hatches to be kept open without jeopardising security, and visual or working access to vulnerable parts of a vessel, bring real conservation benefits.

ADAPTATIONS FOR COMFORT AND CONVENIENCE

The decision to make adaptations to a vessel's fabric merely for the comfort and convenience of the owner should be avoided where possible. However, in some cases, good design and a willingness to be creative can provide solutions which will increase the comfort and convenience for users of an historic vessel without impacting on original fabric. Fifie herring drifter *Reaper*, built in 1901, has had minimal adaptations made to her fabric for comfort and is sailed without the security of guard rails. Her use by a boat club makes this possible, whereas commercial chartering would have made such rails a requirement. One way to maintain authenticity in this situation would be to have removable lifelines fitted as guard rails, so that these can be set up or taken off depending on the purpose for which the vessel is putting to sea.

Helen Smitton is a 38 foot (11.6m) Watson lifeboat, currently undergoing conservation. While in service, she was either housed undercover or, if returning from a rescue, drained of all water as she was winched up the slip. Once reconstructed, she will be kept afloat for most of the year, causing freshwater to collect at the lowest point of the deck, around the engine box coamings. Therefore, she will be discretely adapted to fit her new use, with small drains inserted at six points where freshwater will naturally collect. These will be connected to a pumping chamber with submersible pump and float switch. The pump will discharge at the stern via a swan neck and the chamber will have a sealed lid so that water cannot enter the vessel interior via the drains or pump outlet.

ADAPTATION
a quick guide

7.4

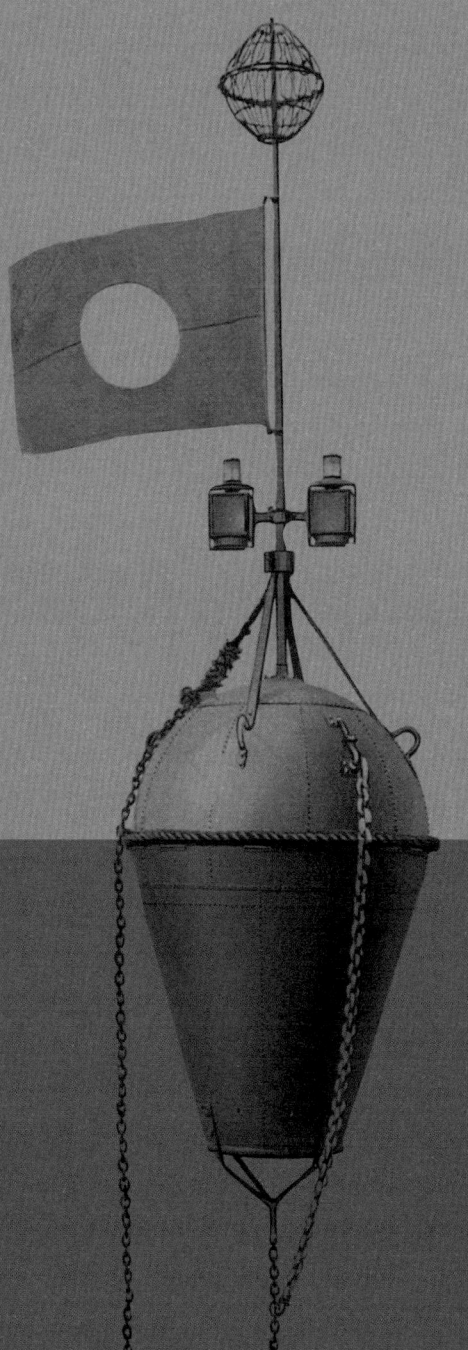

Adaptation is only acceptable when it has minimal impact on the significance of a vessel and makes an essential contribution to sustainability or safety.

Adaptation is most often applied to historic vessels being considered for operational use or as the best means of providing safe visitor access to a static vessel.

Adaptation should be adopted once all other alternatives have been seriously considered and not as a means of making convenient changes.

Query whether the proposed adaptation meets with good conservation practice and whether its impact can be minimised through design.

ADAPTATION CASE STUDY | WILL & FANNY KIRBY

7.4

WILL & FANNY KIRBY

Will & Fanny Kirby was a lifeboat on active service from 1963 to 1993 at Seaham and then Flamborough. Since retirement, she has been displayed as one of the lifeboat collection at Chatham Historic Dockyard. She forms part of the Oakley 37' class, of which there are still a significant number of other representatives surviving, including *J G Graves of Sheffield* – the first of its kind to be built and also on display at Chatham. As *Will & Fanny Kirby* was not a unique survivor and did not have a particularly significant history, the decision was taken to adapt her for interpretation purposes.

An intervention was made to the hull, which stripped a section of the vessel back to the frames. This has been designed both to allow visitors to see inside, but also to reveal her construction. The cut-away illustrates the Oakley self-righting process which was innovative, though not wholly successful as a design feature. The combination of sea water with aluminium and steel parts acted as a corrosive battery and, due to the design, the ballast tanks could never be fully flushed out. For this reason, the Royal National Lifeboat Institution (RNLI) decided that once the Oakleys' service life was ended, these lifeboats should not go back on the water – which remains a condition of their sale to this day.

The design of the current adaptation preserves *Will & Fanny Kirby's* framing, which allows her hull to be 'read' as an uninterrupted structure whilst providing a window onto the complexity of her interior and construction. This is a major gain in presentation relative to the pain of removing part of her original fabric, particularly in the context of a collection of lifeboats where diverse methods of presentation build up a good picture of the type for visitors. An adaptation of this kind adds value to the visitor experience, allowing them to better understand the overall design. However, it can be a controversial conservation process to adopt. In this case, former crew members initially felt that the adaptation did not show the vessel in the right light, as its crew had won two RNLI Bronze medals. This illustrates the strong feeling of empathy which people have for historic vessels and underlines the importance of choosing the right conservation route to best interpret and present the vessel.

8

REPLICATION

REPLICATION

REPLICATION MEANS STARTING FROM SCRATCH TO BUILD A COPY OF A VESSEL AND CAN BE DEFINED AT VARIOUS LEVELS OF DETAIL AND ACCURACY

Above: Working Sail has built a number of replica pilot cutters to date, all based on the lines plans of vessels like these from the Isles of Scilly.

Previous double page spread: Replica pilot cutter, Agnes, *launched in 2003 and built to the lines of the original Isles of Scilly pilot cutter* Agnes *of 1841.*

The relationship between conservation and replication is not unique to historic vessels. Industrial and transport items such as planes, motor cars, railway stock and engines have all seen projects from time to time which seek to create new examples of former technologies. This can occur when there are few or none of these technologies surviving or if there is a strong desire to demonstrate them and the surviving originals are incapable of operation. The general term 'replica' is frequently used to describe all such projects, failing to identify the gradations of replication which carry different levels of accuracy. These gradations have consequential differing impacts on those who construct, fund, or experience the outcome of such initiatives.

Motivation, levels of available information and the use to which the object is to be put will all influence accuracy or the extent to which there is a need to create something which is a faithful reproduction of the original item. An extreme example of the need to create impression rather than accuracy is a stage set, where the method of construction, materials used and level of detail are secondary to the overall effect required. In this case, it is perfectly acceptable to create an impression through a mix of artful construction and 'trompe-l'oeuil'.

However, if the motivation behind a project is to develop a proper appreciation of what something was really like and how it was used, then accuracy of information and painstaking attention to detail become paramount. The aims behind a ship replication project are as crucial in defining how the project is to be taken forward as the decisions taken about the most appropriate route for a particular conservation project, identified at the conservation gateway explained in this book. Conservation and creating a new example of a particular vessel come together when the best way to keep what survives, and develop meaning and understanding from that survival, is deemed to be through stabilising and preserving the original and building afresh.

This chapter sets out to establish clear and workable definitions which will inform decisions where recreation of the vessel is an objective. These distinctions are not academic.

Lizzie May, *a replica pilot cutter, built in 1998 and now acting as a charter boat in the Western Isles of Scotland.*

They determine the nature and depth of the experience for those encountering the vessel and have a bearing on the interest in such a project, thereby potentially affecting the flow of funds available to create and maintain what is built. The Heritage Lottery Fund's policy is not to fund replica projects. At present, other funding bodies are also hesitant to support replication. If the latter can be confident that a new-build project before them is properly defined, they may be open to funding not only fully fledged totally accurate replicas, but also experimental vessel projects designed to extend knowledge and based on incomplete but rigorously analysed 'archaeological' evidence.

TRUE REPLICA

A true replica involves building an exact and complete reproduction of the original vessel. The motivation for such a project might be that no original examples remain, or that what does survive is so rare, delicate, or incomplete that it should be conserved as a reference point from which a new vessel can be built. In doing this, some less significant elements

REPLICATION

Facing page: Eric Nordevall II *is a replica of the paddle steamer built in 1836 to operate on the Gota Canal and named after her engineer. She sank 20 years later and, when the wreck was found 45 metres deep in 1980, it was uniquely well conserved. It was extensively investigated and recorded, allowing a true replica to be built. The replica was constructed as closely to the original as possible, even being endowed with a boiler and engines of the same model as those from 1836, constructed and installed by the same company. The replica has been financed with grant aid from sponsors and members of the non-profit organisation responsible for the build.*

may have to be surmised – for example, minor operational details such as the design of rope fenders, or decorative furnishings such as tiller handle carvings or accommodation furniture. Apart from this, a true replica demonstrably must be a faithful copy of the original.

The level of accuracy required to meet this demanding standard can only be achieved through extensive, verified documentary evidence, by having the original vessel as a 'quarry' for information, or both. Documentary evidence will take the form of line drawings, general arrangement drawings, rigging plans, builder's amendment drawings and notebooks, correspondence, photographs and paintings (where the artist or recorder is known to be an accurate observer of maritime detail). If the original vessel survives, it can only be treated as a source for accurate constructional detail when the nature of that construction can be seen clearly and accurately recorded. In some instances, construction details may be obvious. In others, partial or total deconstruction may be required in order to access the necessary knowledge to achieve a full replica. Should deconstruction be called for, the vessel concerned should be recorded and then deconstructed under National Historic Ships' guidelines.[27] When using the vessel itself as the main source of information, those building the new craft must be very clear on the aims of the project – whether the replica is of the vessel as found, or of the vessel as originally built – and be sure that the information is available to match the project's declared aims.

A vessel does not have to be constructed using the methods and tools of the time in order to achieve the status of a true replica. The key issue is that the new construction conforms to the as found or original intent, design and form of the vessel being replicated. It is perfectly acceptable to use power tools in carrying out the work, and an argument can be mounted in certain circumstances for using modern equivalents for metal hull fastenings where it is not possible to recreate the originals or where there is an issue of longevity. These do not alter form. However, it would not be appropriate to use modern metal fastenings in place of treenails or to use steel rather than iron fittings, both of which are fundamental elements of construction. Similarly, where rigged, a true replica should incorporate original rigging and sail cloth materials: natural fibres have very different performance, visual, and tactile characteristics from those which are man-made.

It must be understood that, in choosing original rigging and materials, the cordage and cloth available today may not be of the quality of the past. The choice of natural fibre cloth and cordage brings with it a much greater need for maintenance, and frequently a faster renewal rate than synthetic imitations of natural materials. However, these problems may in themselves bring useful insights to past practice and performance.

27. Kentley, Stephens & Heighton, *Understanding Historic Vessels* (2007)

The choice of timber to build a true replica, especially those which involve a wooden hull and laid timber deck is not a simple matter. Plainly the first choice should be to find the same type of timber as was used in the original, but this might not always be possible. International regulations on sustainable timbers severely (and rightly) restrict the use of depleted hardwoods from world sources, whilst the stock of mature UK hardwoods is very low. Recycling timber is one way to approach this scarcity (especially with laid teak decks), or use of timbers with similar characteristics – Spanish oak instead of English oak for example. Where lack of availability or cost prevents this, other timbers may be sourced, providing they do not compromise the characteristics or appearance of the true replica being constructed.

There are variants from true replicas in the maritime and non-maritime worlds which derive from the revival of past forms and designs using modern materials and practices where these bring benefits to the original. These should be viewed as being continuous

REPLICATION

Facing page: An operational replica of Captain Cook's famous ship of discovery, HMB Endeavour, *is berthed at the Australian National Maritime Museum. The replica was based on research of original documentation and plans held at the National Maritime Museum, Greenwich. Traditional timber was difficult to source when building the replica, so a West Australian hardwood, 'jarrah', was used. The ship's traditional iron fittings were handmade in a specially installed blacksmith's shop. Traditional manila rope was also handmade on a 140 year old ropewalk to the exact specification of the original standing rigging, but modern polyester was used for the running rigging. As an operational vessel meeting modern regulations, engines, generators, an electric galley, showers and safety equipment were all installed, but were hidden from general view in the cargo hold where Cook stored his ship's provisions.*

design developments gaining from new approaches and materials, not attempts to build faithful copies of past technologies. An outstanding non-maritime example of this is the steam railway engine *Tornado*, completed in 2008. This engine has been built to the original designs of the Peppercorn A1 Pacific Class which it represents, but using elements of modern production methods and specification where appropriate. These include additional water capacity and railway safety electronics, and most notably a welded boiler (constructed in Poland) rather than a riveted one as was the case with the other engines of its class. The project team which built this superb engine are clear that it is not a replica: rather the latest example of what, in the heyday of steam, was a famous and prolific locomotive class. They have given it an official engine number – 60163 and production number 50 in recognition that this locomotive is the direct successor to the 49 built by British Rail in 1948/49. Maritime parallels include the large number of new Cornish gig boats now being built (although production never ceased in the way that railway steam engines did) and, most recently, the building of a new generation of Scottish east coast skiffs by the Scottish Fisheries Museum.

Given the rigorous requirements and demands placed on a true replica, it will come as no surprise that such projects are extremely rare worldwide. The challenge of building a true replica grows with the size and complexity of the vessel: it is simpler to build a true replica of a vessel such as the River Dee salmon boat built in Chester in 1980 for the Merseyside Maritime Museum than a fully-rigged ship. Whatever the size, in cases where these exacting standards have been achieved, the resulting vessel can be a wonderful resource for understanding the original. A true replica gives all those who come in contact with it the thrill which arises from an awareness that huge commitment has gone into creating this vessel, and that what is being witnessed is the next best thing to the original.

The Scandinavian countries have a notable record in the construction of true replicas and hypotheses vessels (see *Hypothesis* below). The Viking Ship Museum in Oslo is home to the famous *Gokstad Ship*, the remarkably complete remains of which were excavated from a Viking burial chamber in Sandar, Norway in 1880. The reconstructed hull of this vessel was the subject of replication in 1893 and several times since, with the *Gaia* (built 1989/90 in Bjorkedalan, Norway) demonstrating the characteristics of a true replica. Even here, some elements of the rig were the subject of research and interpretation (fragments of the sail survived but informed decisions had to be made on the size of the original) and it could be argued that this is a hull replica rather than a true replica (see *Hull Replica* below). Examples of true replicas include the 19th Century Swedish lake steamer *Nordevall* (under completion at the time of writing) and in the UK, the Lerret project given in this publication as a case study, and the cutter built to hang from the davits of HMS *Victory*.

8

REPLICATION

HULL REPLICA

It is not uncommon for a hull or the lines drawings, general arrangement plans and other drawings of a hull to survive, but not the rig or rigging plans. It may also be the case that rig and rigging were radically altered throughout its life (often as a result of the captain's predilections), but that these changes were not recorded. Where vessels have survived, the upper works – masts, spars and rigging – tend to be the first features to deteriorate and vanish, with the hull the last to go. Hulls can survive for generations lying alongside quay walls, in mud and in silt, or completely buried by accident or design.

Given this, it is possible to have sufficient, verified information to build an accurate replica of the hull of a vessel, but not the rig. Depending on the importance of the vessel and the interest it generates, there may be an argument for building a true hull replica with the rig shown as a notional arrangement. Where this is done, it is vital that the notional aspects are differentiated from the true replica hull so that there can be no confusion.

OPERATIONAL REPLICA

An operational replica is a replica vessel where the original design has been adapted to meet modern-day health and safety, Maritime and Coastguard Agency (MCA), and international regulations, allowing the vessel to operate within carefully defined parameters. Vessels seeking limited operational capability (such as being able to visit UK ports where they then become static exhibits but do not take passengers) may face only minimal changes (for example, the addition of guard rails, or installation of modern navigation equipment). Those looking to carry large numbers of passengers or to voyage further afield may be required to make extensive changes to the original design (for example: welded rather than riveted hulls; bigger hull volumes; additional bulkheads; the addition of engines – in the case of sailing vessels – or different specifications for power units). Such adaptations can materially compromise the essential characteristics of the original vessel upon which the intended operational replica is to be based. In these circumstances, the project objectives should be reviewed and may be better achieved through the construction of a 'representation' (see below).

An excellent example of a rigorously thought-through operational replica is the Australian-built *Endeavour* berthed at the Australian National Maritime Museum in Sydney. Great care has been taken to recreate the hull form of Captain Cook's ship, with the rig as close as possible to the original ship even down to the use of hemp rope. The lower deck (mess deck and galley, midshipmen and mates mess, officers' cabins) and the afterfall (gentlemen's quarters, officers' Mess, Great Cabin) maintain their original dimensions. However, concessions to the demands placed on the ship in taking people to sea today have been made by creating a '20th Century Deck' in the hold, with raised headroom, showers, galley, fridge-freezers for a long voyage, and engine room.

HYPOTHESIS

A hypothesis vessel project is one where historical and technical information is available at a level that is sufficient to allow a vessel to be built which can test theories, but which cannot be guaranteed as being a faithful recreation. Sources of information for such projects may include: the incomplete remains of extant vessels; the outcomes from rigorously undertaken archaeological excavations; contemporary paintings or illustrations such as tomb paintings and reliefs; manuscripts; models (including votive models held in churches); similar vessels which survive; incomplete vessel plans; photographs and drawings; crew lists and bills of lading, and written descriptions. Proponents of these projects must demonstrate that such sources have been the subject of disciplined analysis and informed research techniques in order to ensure that the hypothesis being drawn from the evidence stands up to scrutiny.

Those leading the project also need to understand that what is gleaned from such information is not definitive, that the build programme is experimental and that changes in detail along the way are almost certain to be required.

Sea Stallion, *a rigorously researched hypothesis replica, is made of oak and measures almost 30 metres long by 3.8 metres wide. A crew of 100 volunteers sailed this ship to Dublin from Denmark.*

REPLICATION

HM Schooner Pickle, *seen here under sail, is an operational hypothesis. She is a replica based on the vessel commanded by Lieutenant Lapenotiere at the Battle of Trafalgar 1805.*

Hypothesis projects can offer a great deal by way of extending technical and historical knowledge through experimentation, for instance, how these vessels may have been rigged (or powered by other means), crewed and handled, the nature and level of onboard mechanical aids such as engines and in some cases, the contribution they may have made in the movement of peoples, exploration, or trade.

Hypothesis projects have been predicated on vessels from all ages. Very often they relate to earlier periods when documentary evidence is limited and many are archaeologically based. A good example of a rigorously undertaken hypothesis project can be found in the research project to build *Sea Stallion*, the hypothetical construction of a Longship from the Dublin area, built in 1042 and deliberately sunk near Skuldelev in the Roskilde fjord at the end of the 11th Century to protect the harbour there. The hypothesis was built in Roskilde at the Vikingeskibsmuseet using tools recreated from the Viking era which (significantly from a modern perspective) did not include saws, the planks of the original boat being split to achieve the required thickness. Upon completion, *Sea Stallion* was sailed and rowed to Dublin in 2007 by 65 volunteers. Other well-known projects based on experimental archaeology or ethnography with minimal modern interventions include Thor Heyerdahl's *Kon Tiki* and *Ra II*, Tim Severin's open hide boat *Brendon*, and *Olympias*, the 1987 Greek Trireme project.

8

OPERATIONAL HYPOTHESIS

An operational hypothesis is a vessel which has been the subject of considered research to determine as closely as possible from limited information how the original was configured and which is then constructed on the basis of that research, but (as with an operational replica), adapted to meet operational requirements. There are many examples of operational hypotheses around the world. Two well known ones in the UK are the adapted 1996 St. Petersburg-built HM Schooner *Pickle*, the ship which carried the news of the Battle of Trafalgar and *Matthew*, the 1997 replica of the late medieval carrack in which John Cabot voyaged from Bristol to Newfoundland.

REPRESENTATIONS

Vessels which are representations draw on known features from a vessel type and might or might not take on the appearance of a specific vessel. Where there is an intention to represent a particular vessel, research (perhaps from secondary rather than primary sources) may be undertaken but the emphasis is on overall impression not accuracy. Construction often involves modern techniques and cosmetic additions, for example, mock rivets applied to a welded hull. Hull form may be changed to meet operational requirements (for instance, hull volume, placing of bulkheads, accommodation). Other modern attributes (wiring, fire alarms, plumbing systems) are often hidden by internal features such as saloon panelling, false ceilings and false decks.

The intention behind a representation is critical to the outcome. There are excellent representations of historic vessels designed for the nostalgia market – for example, steam and motor launches with fibreglass hulls, modern power units built to period appearance, and modern fittings such as marine-ply panelling or electric lights. Larger commercial craft are being built as ferries and trip boats to evoke the feeling of an age: Edwardian and Art Deco are consistently popular. Sailing vessels built for cruising or sail training may take generic form, or features from specific ships, but are often not designed to closely replicate the vessel from which such features have been taken.

All such representations have their place, but they must not be confused with replicas or hypothesis vessels which have been the subject of rigorous research and construction under heritage principles.

The Matthew *is an operational hypothesis of 15th Century mapmaker and explorer John Cabot's ship. She is based on generic designs of ships from the period and her dimensions were calculated from her tonnage and the number of her crew – the only known details of her specification. She has an engine and full cooking facilities.*

REPLICATION CASE STUDY | LERRET

8

LERRET

Gail McGarva is a traditional wooden boat builder, trained at the Lyme Regis Boat Building Academy. Her current project is to build a replica of the last seaworthy lerret, *Vera*, a traditional working boat built in 1923 and used to catch mackerel with a seine net off the steeply shelved Chesil Beach. The lerret is a double-ended, flat floored, beamy clinker craft which relied on its inherent strength and buoyancy to be launched and beached rapidly through the surf without being swamped. Gail has been awarded a scholarship from the Queen Elizabeth Trust to build a traditional lerret, using the hull of *Vera* to create a replica vessel.

Gail's first step was to measure the existing hull of *Vera* and take references for three mould positions, at the points where the boat changes shape significantly. From these dimensions, she was able to create three working moulds. The replica will be built using the same beam, length and timbers as the original vessel, with elm planking of the same thickness, an oak backbone and twelve planks per side. However, Gail will be working alongside Roy Gollop, one of the few boat builders in Dorset who still builds 'by eye'. Because *Vera's* 17 foot (5.18 metre) hull remains intact, some of the analysis of fabric has proved difficult. Gail and Roy will need to use an element of judgment in the build, for example, in the ways the planks divide or when sighting the sheer line in sympathy to the hull as it evolves. The replica will be built largely using traditional tools and materials.

However, whilst the hull will be copper riveted as with the original, Gail will use glue for the scarf joints.

An understanding of *Vera*, the existing hull, has been reached via a mixture of both off-ship research and fabric analysis. Gail has undertaken considerable research into the history of lerrets, creating a growing archive of documents, stories and photographs from survivors who both worked and restored these vessels. She discovered that whilst the inherent characteristics of the lerret remain the same in all craft of this type, there is often a variation in the details of build. Equally, in some cases, distortions may have developed in the shape during the vessel's life or original plank lines may not be fair. In this way, by using builder's judgment in certain places, they achieve a vessel that gives a sense of lineage, but still has a life of its own. As Gail explains, she is creating a 'daughtership', based on the fabric of *Vera*.

The build project is running over a 10 month period and, upon completion, the replica will be launched alongside the 'mothership', so the two vessels can be seen afloat together. Funding permitting, Gail will then be researching twelve stories across Dorset relating to lerret history, for inclusion in an oral history book and website. In the meantime, *Vera* is on static display and ultimately will become a working exhibit, whilst the replica lerret will be used for sail training and to carry the reality of the work of Chesil fisher folk on to future generations.

9 MAINTENANCE

9 ensuring longterm survival

MAINTENANCE

MAINTENANCE MEANS THE CONTINUOUS PROTECTIVE CARE OF THE FABRIC OF A VESSEL AND SHOULD BE DISTINGUISHED FROM REPAIR, WHICH INVOLVES RESTORATION OR RECONSTRUCTION

Previous double page spread: Passenger vessel Alaska *was discovered in 1974, decked over with plywood and filled with concrete, in use as a boarding pontoon for other hire boats. After conservation, she is now maintained for operational use and in 2009 was chosen as a 'royal barge', taking Queen Elizabeth II for a cruise on the Thames.*

Maintenance slows down the natural deterioration of materials and should be the first priority for any historic vessel owner. A period of inadequate maintenance followed by major works increases the costs and also wipes out original fabric that could have been kept if a vessel had been well maintained. Whatever her environment, whether carefully supported in a museum under cover, or taken around Cape Horn by her owner, a regime of routine inspection and maintenance should be appropriate to a vessel's condition when first established, but will need regular updates. It should also be reviewed if there are changes either to the vessel's environment or to her fabric.

Good maintenance is costly, but lack of maintenance or work done badly is far more expensive. Failures that are noted and then put right at an early stage cost less than leaving them until a later date when the deterioration will be worse. Inadequate maintenance shortens the lives of historic boats and ships and can result in total loss. Maintenance costs are notoriously difficult to judge and are usually under-estimated. In some cases, there are ways of reducing these. Fifie *Reaper* is kept in working order at the Scottish Fisheries Museum and regularly sailed to regattas. Her maintenance costs are substantially lessened by experienced and dedicated volunteers who undertake some of her upkeep for free, thereby reducing the costs of annual winter work in a boatyard. The expertise of these enthusiasts and a good working relationship with the boatyard means that the specification for winter work can also be discussed in detail and carried out exactly as needed.

The size of vessel has important implications for the maintenance regime. The decision to add fabric to any historic vessel needs to be assessed in advance, not only on the grounds of conservation ethics, but in the light of any additional maintenance burden it will bring. For very large vessels, the distance to a suitable dock for periodic haul-outs to inspect and undertake maintenance below the waterline, and the type of waters she will encounter travelling there, will impact on the condition in which she needs to be kept. In 1971, HMS *Belfast* was brought to the Pool of London having been saved from the breakers' yard. Some work was undertaken in the expectation that she would never have to leave the Thames Estuary again, for example, the refurbishment or replacement of all her waste

9

Watercolours by artist William Payne, 1815, showing the paying of a ship.

and drainage scupper valves in plastic. In 1982, she was dry docked at Tilbury for cleaning, shot-blasting and necessary repairs. Tilbury New Dry Dock, London's last remaining dock facility, closed in the late 1980s and dry docking since has forced her back to sea. This has significant financial implications arising from towage and also impacts on the maintenance and repairs needed to put her into a condition to obtain a license to enter the Channel.

There are a number of modern devices available that can make maintenance more efficient, especially in large complex ships where some spaces may be awkward to inspect. Monitoring equipment, including remote monitors for humidity and moisture content in materials, has become more sophisticated and provides effective and reliable checking and warning systems at low cost. Equipment of this kind, however, should never be regarded as a substitute for good human observation. The human eyes and nose, when properly used, continue to be the most efficient tools for seeking out problems and no mechanical device can arrange swift remedial action. Many vessels known to have sunk have done so at their own moorings and this underlines the value of a warning system, regular human presence and recurrent use of vessels being kept for operational purposes.

MAINTENANCE

PRESERVED BOATS AND SHIPS

Once a vessel has been conserved, she still needs to be maintained, whether for operational use or static display. Norfolk & Suffolk sailing and pulling lifeboat Alfred Corry *has now been conserved and is on display to the public at Southwold. Despite being well protected in a former lifeboat shed, she will still require maintenance and regular inspection to ensure her present condition is upheld.*

Preserved boats and ships kept undercover, where fabric is of prime importance, should have a written 'vessel care plan' incorporating a maintenance regime. This should include regular checks to ensure that support and ventilation are adequate, that the vessel has not suffered from excessive drying out, is not showing signs of structural failure, and is adequately protected from damage, either deliberate or inadvertent, caused by visitors. A cleaning cycle should also be incorporated. Access for cleaning a fragile structure may be difficult and bring a risk of mechanical damage to the vessel. There should be a clear understanding of who is responsible for cleaning, adequate training if required and appropriate products and appliances made available. The care plan should include monitoring the environment in which a vessel is kept and, where possible, adjusting to keep deterioration to a minimum. Engines of significance fitted to preserved vessels should be turned over at regular intervals to prevent them seizing up.

VESSELS KEPT AFLOAT – AS STATIC EXHIBITS OR IN OPERATIONAL USE

For floating vessels, a structured maintenance plan will be needed which should include regular hull inspections, an annual fit-out above and below decks and, where relevant, checks on the means of propulsion. Maintenance must keep the hull watertight, as well as protecting both it and the deck or superstructure from rot caused by rainwater and spray. The hull of any floating vessel will need cyclical inspection and treatment, allowing for recaulking wooden vessels below the waterline, cleaning rust gently off metal boats and checking cathodic protection systems. Any fittings that pass through the hull, like pump outlets, should also be checked. For decked vessels, inspection and maintenance should ensure that water runs off the deck and overboard. There is no point dealing with the effects of a leak if its source has not been identified and put right. Any hollows in the fabric where water can collect and stand should be corrected and drains and scuppers checked meticulously.

Water in the bilges will generate a humid atmosphere, damaging to fabric. For larger vessels left unattended, bilge alarms and automatic bilge pumps are vital to deal with small leaks and avoid disasters. However, these may leave water in the bilges which could encourage corrosion. They may also disguise a problem from the owner who may not realise how often they are activated in his or her absence. To ensure that there are no leaks it is essential that the bilges are pumped as often as possible. They should be kept dry, even if it means mopping out the last drops by hand. While this is tiresome, it ensures that there are no free surfaces from which water can evaporate, and spread dampness.

Temporary and winter covers are extremely valuable for vessels kept in the open air, so long as they do not conflict with the need for good ventilation. Adequate ventilation for internal spaces should be provided at all times. Clutter anywhere in the vessel, but particularly in the bilges, creates condensation and humidity as well as obscuring problems. Ventilators should be checked to make sure they are working. Locking access hatches and fitting them with portable ventilators which can be locked down are simple and inexpensive procedures. Depending on the size of the compartments, two ventilators per compartment, one high-set through the deck and one trunked to the lowest part ensures good circulation of air throughout. Varnished spars benefit from protection from the sunlight when not in use.

Regular inspection and renewal of coatings for a vessel that is not preserved undercover are important, and have the advantage of alerting an owner to deterioration of metal or wood at an early stage as well as ensuring maximum protection of fabric. Wood should be treated with a suitable rot proofer and should not be painted with impervious coatings until it is dry. This prevents rot flourishing in a damp microclimate between layers of paint and will ensure that paint adheres properly. However, rot-proofers can be problematical in their application and can hamper later repairs where glues and compounds (traditional or modern) are used. Careful consideration should be given before adopting rot-proofing as a solution. Where metal has corroded the rust has to be removed, by hand or with power tools and by applying a paint manufacturer's full specification, including a corrosion inhibitor. The surface should be treated with an anti-corrosive treatment and a complete paint scheme. There are some quick anti-corrosive treatments that give a good protection, but may make it more difficult to apply paint adequately afterwards.

Modern paint coatings may not provide the most appropriate finish for historic vessels (although, carefully chosen, such coatings can give long-term protection for steel and iron). Those which are irreversible or non-removable should be avoided. Glass reinforced plastic (GRP), rubber and vinyl products are not suitable for decks unless there is a historic precedent for them. Equally, GRP or other non-reversible modern products are not appropriate coatings for traditional wooden hulls. They may shorten the life of a boat by concealing and accelerating decay.

For operational vessels, regular inspection and a written maintenance plan is essential. Fifie Reaper *is seen here being launched after a re-fit in 2008.*

MAINTENANCE

Facing page: This oil painting by John Everett shows sails spread out on the deck of the barque, Birkdale, *being repaired whilst on passage to Texas in 1920.*

In addition to covers, the relationship between a vessel and her environment should be adjusted where possible as part of her maintenance programme. Changing her ballast helps to reduce rot and rust at the waterline. Regular turning ensures even weathering. Moorings must be inspected on a regular basis, with care taken to ensure adequate and appropriate fendering to remove the ever-present danger of damage from banging and chafing. For vessels temporarily undercover, raising the temperature and dehumidifying the environment will retard rust and rot. When vessels are kept outside, the area underneath should be clear of rubbish. However, grass can be of benefit as it restricts the flow of damaging warm air in the summer and evaporating moisture keeps the hull tight. Good access should be regularly reviewed and, if necessary, better access to vulnerable parts of the vessel should be carefully designed to minimise the impact on fabric. Vessels where paying passengers or the general public come onboard will need elements designed for the health and safety of visitors kept in good order as part of the regular maintenance regime.

Rig and sails require just as frequent maintenance, whether the vessel is static or operational. Natural fibre cordage requires regular treatment and 'end for ending' to reduce chafe and in the case of static vessels to diminish 'rot spots'. Wire rigging requires dressing and sails need careful overhauling and protection from ultra violet light (UV). Even if a synthetic option has been taken for rigging, it still needs regular care and maintenance, especially as some of the synthetic imitations can be very susceptible to chafe and degradation from UV. Polyester, whilst looking more synthetic and increasing costs, tends to have greater resistance.

PROCEDURES SPECIFIC TO VESSELS IN OPERATIONAL USE

Ships and boats in operational use need one set of regular maintenance checks when being used and another when they are unmanned. Operational vessels laid up ashore for winter should be checked on a monthly basis. If laid up afloat, moorings, covers, hatches, port holes etc. must be inspected more frequently and ideally, if vessels are moored in situations where they are exposed to higher risk, on a daily basis. For vessels subject to Maritime and Coastguard Agency (MCA) inspection it makes sense to develop the maintenance programme around the external inspection cycles and the external requirements for haul-out. For vessels in use, a working logbook should be maintained on board. Ideally, all entries should then be copied to a master file ashore, where they can be checked against the maintenance plan which can be amended accordingly if required.

Moving parts of machinery should be treated with suitable waterproof lubricants and

engines should be turned over weekly. There is a very comprehensive range of long term lubricants, wax type coatings, and anti-corrosive materials on the market. It is well worth looking for suppliers or manufacturers who can give technical advice and good discounts for historic vessels. Be wary of using a quick protective on a surface which will eventually be painted, as it may be difficult to remove and prevent adherence of the paint. Fuel, water, and lubrication systems demand regular maintenance checks and may need draining, then inspection for leaks and corrosion. Filters will require cleaning or changing. Fuel tanks are liable to collect condensed water, which can do a lot of damage and cause engine failure. Bilges can collect an evil mix of water and oils and must be inspected and drained. Diesel tanks should have sumps, through which water can be drained. Where possible and safe, keep fuel tanks full of fuel. Compressed air, electrical systems and lifting gear may require professional inspection if certification is to be kept updated.

INSPECTIONS

A formal maintenance plan is highly desirable however the vessel is to be conserved, whether afloat, in the open ashore or under cover. More regular inspection will be needed of areas where there is known degradation, but which are not yet bad enough to require treatment. Parts of vessels afloat which are at high risk, such as the wind and water regions, will need their own considered inspection regime. Alternatively, readily accessible dry areas which are not subject to much wear and tear will need little inspection. Rates of degradation of different materials should be considered. A properly laid-out plan and timeline will ensure that nothing important is forgotten, whilst keeping the time needed for inspections to a minimum.

OBSERVATIONS

The written maintenance programme should clearly state who is responsible for all elements of maintenance. This is essential when the care of an historic vessel is managed by a group or groups of people. Nobody involved in the management or care of a historic boat or ship should be excluded from her maintenance. Everyone, including volunteers when they are part of an organisation, should be formally trained to be observant and report any failures or problems identified. These should be recorded and the single person or group specifically set up to deal with maintenance should examine the records and create a list of action points in order of priority.

MAINTENANCE
a quick guide

9

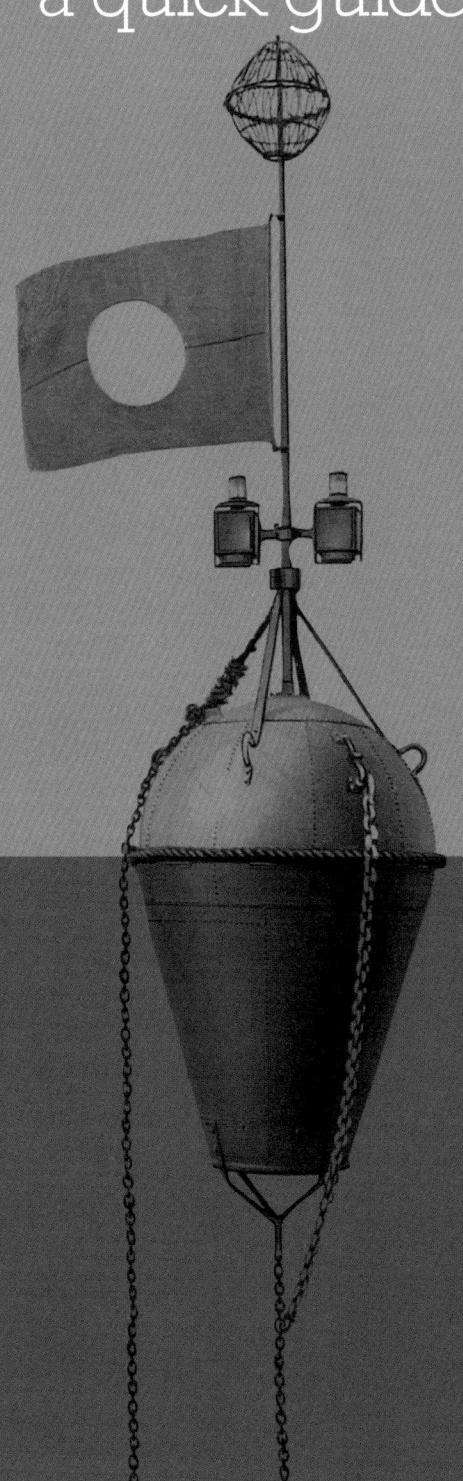

Regular maintenance is the key to the conservation of historic vessels, but differs from restoration or reconstruction which involve major repairs.

Adjusting or controlling the environment in which a vessel is kept to provide a moisture content level in-keeping with their long term care and protection will help with overall maintenance and reduce the risk of fungal and insect infestation.

Maintenance should be managed by devising and implementing a costed regime on an annual basis, customised according to a vessel's materials, design, condition, environment and use.

Manufacturers' recommended maintenance cycles should be followed for all equipment, including fire-fighting, safety and security equipment.

Operating vessels should comply with external regulations for maintenance.

Salt water is a natural and freely available biocide, effective in reducing rot in wooden decks and fittings. Washing down with it is a simple and effective method of maintaining wooden vessels. However, it can be very damaging to metal vessels, parts or fittings.

In some cases appropriate use of modern techniques and materials can reduce costs without damage to significance.

MAINTENANCE CASE STUDY | WESTERNMAN

9

WESTERNMAN

Westernman is a 40 foot (12.19 metre) representation of a Bristol Channel pilot cutter, built of wood epoxy in 1997 for private owners, Tom & Ros Cunliffe. She is in regular operational use and has a rolling maintenance cycle which allows her to remain in commission all year round. As part of this, Tom hauls her out for a week long refit at the start of each season. Her hull is power-hosed off and given a fresh coat of antifouling. Tom takes the opportunity to check the underwater fittings, such as the anodes and propeller in case of electrolysis. Cutless bearings, rudder pintles and the general condition of the bottom are also looked at, with any action taken at this stage. To coincide with the haul-out, the mast and spars are removed from the boat every two years. A complete standing and running rig overhaul is undertaken which includes servicing the 55 wooden blocks. The spars are stripped, sanded and finished with a minimum 7 coats of oil. The spars are oiled in situ between services. *Westernman* is usually put on a drying berth in mid-season, or hoisted in the SeaLift, to keep the bottom clean, if the waters she is cruising have caused any fouling.

As part of the spring refit, the standing rigging is slushed with a 50/50 mix of Stockholm tar and boiled linseed oil and the dead-eyes 'set up'. All blocks are sanded and oiled, using the Norwegian oil, *Varnol*, which allows for easy touch-up during the season. Ros fully services all brightwork including hatches, capping, pin rails and cavels in Spring. This may involve stripping, but is often a case of a rub down and a couple of coats of *Varnol*. A further application is mandatory in Autumn, before the Winter sets in, but removable

CASE STUDY | WESTERNMAN

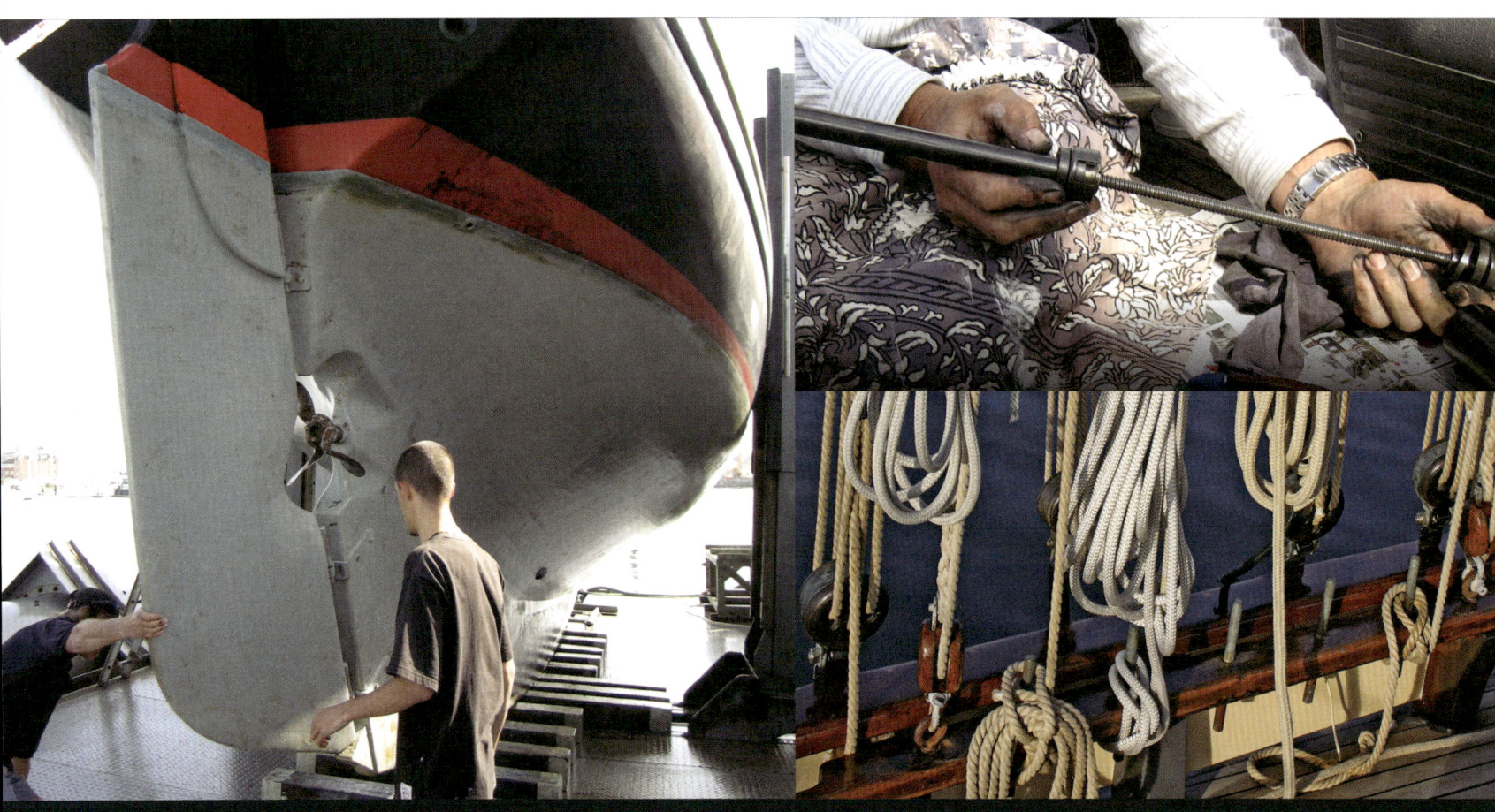

covers are fitted for the main and fore hatch, the cockpit/companionway and the mainsail which are in place when not cruising. This gives added protection to the varnish and lessens the maintenance impact, as does washing down the brightwork with fresh water after any hard sail, to ensure that the salt residue is removed and won't cause deterioration.

The paintwork on deck is re-done, or patched, annually, but the topsides every 2 or 3 years. Tom is careful not to do this too often, or put the paint on too thickly, as a build up of multiple layers would shorten the periods between stripping right back. Down below, Ros paints a cabin each year: ensuring a regular rotation keeps the boat looking smart, but the maintenance within achievable boundaries. She uses vinegar and water to keep the varnish fresh and cleans the painted bulkheads with Milton (sterilising fluid). Tom surveys the rigging keenly and any chafe may mean replacement of ropes, or chafing gear installed to protect the woodwork.

9

Sails are serviced as required, with valeting anticipated every three years (approximately 6,000 miles). Because of the composite construction, and careful selection of sealants, the wooden decks are virtually maintenance free.

Tom is meticulous about checking equipment on board as part of the maintenance programme. The winches are serviced as required, and the anchor chain will be taken off annually, cleaned and inspected to ensure the depth markings are still legible. The liferaft is serviced on a two year basis, and the dates on the flares are checked. Fire extinguishers could need re-filling and all electrics are tested. The filter in the water tanks is renewed regularly, with the tanks themselves emptied and cleaned every 4 or 5 years. The bilge is also cleaned and the engine fully serviced. *Westernman* has sailed over 25,000 nautical miles in the 13 years since build and the regular maintenance has paid off, keeping her ready to go to sea at any time.

MAINTENANCE CASE STUDY | HISTORIC TUG

9

MAINTENANCE CYCLE FOR A HISTORIC TUG IN OPERATIONAL USE

The inspection and maintenance regime should be specific to the vessel. When she is in use there should be a set of daily checks on her systems, machinery, fluid levels and controls.

These should be detailed in an Operational Manual, and could comprise the following series:

1. On first going on board
2. Before sailing
3. Before leaving the vessel, after returning from sea

When she is not operational, she should receive visits at least weekly, starting with visual assessment of the outside of the vessel, her moorings, and access. Other checks should cover the interior, beginning with the bilges in each compartment, recording any water, removing it completely, then going through the machinery and systems, looking at the fluid levels, air pressure for air start machinery, and the state of the batteries.

Depending on the condition of the vessel, the next level could be monthly monitoring or visits every other month, in the course of which all machinery that is operable should be run, batteries and air topped up, and all lights and controls operated, including radios.

A full annual inspection should also be carried out, possibly by the owner, but looking at all the points which would be covered by an MCA surveyor, and a survey report prepared. Arising from this would be a list of defects, which form the basis of the work list for the winter refit. This should include checking the lifesaving and fire-fighting equipment.

Every 4 years, if the vessel remains operational, the annual survey would have to be carried out to full MCA or inland waterways approved standards, which would mean hauling her out of the water. This is a good opportunity for a personal underwater survey, and a repaint of the outside of the hull.

DEFINITIONS

The language of conservation is specialised. Terms that are clearly understood to mean one thing in the conservation of buildings may mean another in the museum world and may be used quite differently in common parlance. This is confusing. In the boat and ship world, for example, the term 'restoration' is frequently applied to any project to get an old boat back in use, whether or not the process respects the age or integrity of the vessel, records what is done to her, or is undertaken with a view to passing on something of her historic integrity to future generations. The key definitions used in this book are set below and specifically relate to conserving historic vessels. If guidance on specialist nautical terminology is required, National Historic Ships has published an online glossary. The Manual of Maritime Curatorship produced by the Maritime Curators Group also offers a select glossary.

Facing page: The wardroom and forward mess deck of an S-Class submarine showing the view through a Davis Escape Chamber, painted by war artist Stephen Bone.

ADAPTATION
means modifying a vessel to suit a proposed new use. Vessels in operational use may need adapting to install required safety equipment, or for practical reasons, for example the provision of a toilet. Vessels that are visited as attractions will need adaptations for visitors on board, each of which requires careful recording.

ASSOCIATIONS
mean the special connections that exist between people or places and a vessel. There may be historic associations between national figures and a vessel. Large groups of people may have associations with a vessel, for example descendents of her crew or descendents of emigrants who travelled in her. People may have a special interest in a vessel that has been, or is, a part of their ethnic or personal history, or a vessel may be intimately associated with a specific place.

CONSERVATION
means all the processes of looking after a vessel so as to sustain her significance and pass this on.

Conservation encompasses maintenance and the processes of preservation, restoration, reconstruction and adaptation. More than one conservation process may be applied to the whole vessel or different parts of her at the same time, or at different times in her life.

Conservation of operational use is likely to sacrifice some original fabric in the short term, and more over the long term. Rigorous conservation of the fabric of a whole vessel will sacrifice part of the design purpose by abandoning operational use.

CONSERVATION MANAGEMENT PLAN
means a document which sets out the significance of a historic vessel, stating how that significance will be retained in any future use, alteration, management or repair. Includes information about the vessel, why it is important, what is happening to it and what policies are in place to manage and maintain it, and to ensure that new work is appropriate. Involves consultation with stakeholders.

FABRIC
means all the physical material of the vessel including structural components and fixtures. The following terms relate to the overall definition of fabric:

> **ORIGINAL FABRIC**
> – the physical materials with which the vessel was originally built
>
> **FABRIC AS FOUND**
> – the physical materials of the vessel at the point of acquisition.

FUNCTION
means the characteristic actions that define the purpose for which a vessel was built (for example, dredger).

HISTORIC VESSEL
means any vessel built over 50 years ago.

HULL REPLICA – see **REPLICATION**

INTERPRETATION

means all the ways of presenting the significance of a vessel to the general public.

Interpretation includes explanations of a vessel's significance to other people, such as an account of her history passed on to the next owner: a website which illustrates and explains her, or graphic panels and guides on board a ship which is a visitor attraction.

MAINTENANCE

means the continuous protective care of the fabric of a vessel. All conserved vessels, whether operational, static afloat or static ashore require ongoing maintenance appropriate for their use and their environment. This does not include restoration, reconstruction or adaptation

NATIONAL HISTORIC FLEET

means all vessels listed on the National Register of Historic Vessels that are deemed of pre-eminent national significance.

OPERATIONAL REPLICA – see **REPLICATION**

OPERATIONAL USE

means a use to which the vessel was put and may vary during its lifetime. Operational use is not the same as purpose. All vessels were designed to fulfil a purpose or several purposes: fighting, fishing, transporting goods or passengers, or for pleasure. Conserving operational use is rarely the same as conserving a vessel's historic purpose.

ORIGINAL FABRIC – see **FABRIC**

PRESERVATION

means keeping the fabric or part of the fabric of a vessel as far as possible in its existing state, and retarding deterioration. Preservation of whole vessels is incompatible with operational use and whole preserved vessels must usually be kept ashore and undercover. Parts of static and operational vessels can be preserved.

RECONSTRUCTION

means returning the fabric or part of the fabric of a vessel to a known earlier state, but is distinguished from restoration by the introduction of new material into the fabric. Reconstruction is the most commonplace conservation process applied to operating vessels.

> **EXTREME RECONSTRUCTION**
>
> means reconstruction where the majority of the original material is decayed or missing, resulting in a major rebuild using new materials.

RELATED PLACE, VESSEL OR OBJECT

means a place, vessel or object that contributes to the significance of the vessel but is elsewhere.

The ship yard in which she was built, or a harbour or boat club with which she has been associated may contribute to the significance of a vessel. Other vessels of the same type, whether surviving or known only by record, may contribute to her significance, as may works of art, paper documentation, or photographic, video and film material.

REPLICATION

means starting from scratch to build a copy of a vessel. Replication in conjunction with preservation can have a legitimate role to play in the wider conservation process. In this context, replication can be a useful way of establishing the appearance, nature and form of an historic vessel, without harming the preservation of the original, which can remain in a protected environment. There are differing levels of replication, which are:

TRUE REPLICA

means building an exact and complete reproduction of the original vessel.

HULL REPLICA

means building an exact replica of the hull of a vessel, but not the rig.

OPERATIONAL REPLICA

means building an accurate replica but with adaptations to meet modern-day health and safety, MCA and international regulations in order to allow the vessel to operate within carefully defined parameters.

HYPOTHESIS

means a theoretical vessel based on archaeological, historical and technical information which can test theories but which cannot be guaranteed as a faithful recreation.

OPERATIONAL HYPOTHESIS

means a theoretical vessel based on archaeological, historical and technical information but with adaptations to meet modern-day health and safety, MCA, and international regulations in order to allow the vessel to operate within carefully defined parameters.

REPRESENTATION

means a vessel which draws on known features from the craft it has been designed to represent, but which may or may not take on the appearance of a specific vessel. The emphasis is on overall impression rather than accuracy.

REPRESENTATION – see **REPLICATION**

RESTORATION

means returning the existing fabric or part of the fabric of a vessel to a known earlier state by removing additions or re-assembling existing components with the minimum introduction of new material and without conjecture.

SETTING

means the surroundings of a static vessel including its visual context.

SIGNIFICANCE

means the sum of the cultural values of a vessel, broadly interpreted. These may be historic, aesthetic, scientific, political, cultural, social or spiritual values for past, present or future generations. Ships and boats may have a range of economic significances for different individuals or groups at different times. Significance is embodied in the vessel itself, as a combination of its fabric, purpose, use, associations, meanings, records, related vessels and places.

STATEMENT OF SIGNIFICANCE
means a formal document, setting out the heritage merit of a vessel, based on the sum of its cultural values.

SUSTAINABLE
means capable of meeting present needs whilst ensuring viability in the future.

TRUE REPLICA – see **REPLICATION**

TYPE
means the structural characteristics that together define the class or group of the vessel (for example, topsail schooner).

VESSEL
means any boat or ship.

WORKING LIFE
is the period during which the vessel was operated for any purpose other than a heritage or museum use. Working life may be limited to part of a particular river or an area associated with a length of coastline, but a vessel with a long working life may have operated in several locations.

WORKING LOCATION
means the area in which the historic vessel operates or operated.

Bibliography

The following is a select bibliography of sources used specifically in the research for this publication. Every effort has been made to ensure references are accurate. However, this is intended as an overview of subject material, rather than an academic resource. Further information can be obtained via the accompanying online bibliography at: www.nationalhistoricships.org.uk

Anderson, Richard K., *Guidelines for Recording Historic Ships*, Historic American Buildings Survey/Historic American Engineering Record (National Park Service, U.S. Department of the Interior, 1988)

Ball, Stephen and Winsor, Peter, *Larger & Working Objects: A guide to their preservation and care* (Museums & Galleries Commission: n.d.)

Bass, George F., (gen. ed.), *A history of Seafaring based on underwater archaeology* (Thames and Hudson: London, 1974)

Billingham, Nick, *Narrow Boats: Care and Maintenance* (Crowood Press: Wiltshire, 2003)

Brock, P.W. and Greenhill, Basil, *Steam and Sail: in Britain and North America* (David & Charles: Newton Abbot, 1973)

Brouwer, Norman J., *International Register of Historic Ships*, Second Edition (Anthony Nelson Ltd: Shropshire, 1993)

Colledge, JJ, *Ships of the Royal Navy: The Complete Record of all Ships of the Royal Navy from the 15th century to the Present*, Volumes I & II (1970, 1989, partly revised edition, 2003)

Conder, Tony, *Canal Narrowboats and Barges* (Shire Publications: 2004)

Corlett, E.C.B., *The Iron Ship* (Conway: London, 1990)

Danenberg, Don, *How To Restore Your Wooden Runabout*, Vol. 2 (Motorbooks: USA, 2005)

Dodds, James and Moore, James, *Building the Wooden Fighting Ship* (Hutchinson: London, 1984)

Elliott, Colin and Jenkins, Ford, *Sailing Fishermen in old photographs* (Tops'l Books: Reading, 1978)

Feilden, Bernard M., *Conservation of Historic Buildings* (Butterworth-Heinemann: Oxford, 1994)

Frost, Ted, *From Tree to Sea: The building of a wooden steam drifter* (Terence Dalton: Suffolk, 2007)

Greenhill, Basil, *A Quayside Camera 1845-1917* (David & Charles: Newton Abbot, 1975)

Greenhill, Basil, *Archaeology of the Boat: A new introductory study* (A. & C. Black: London, 1976)

Greenhill, Basil and Gifford, Ann, *Travelling by Sea in the Nineteenth Century: interior design in Victorian passenger ships* (A. & C. Black: London, 1972)

Greenhill, Basil and Gifford, Ann, *Victorian and Edwardian Sailing Ships from old photographs* (Batsford: London, 1982)

Greenhill, Basil and Gifford, Ann, *Victorian and Edwardian Merchant Steamships from old photographs* (Batsford: London, 1982)

Greenhill, Basil and Mannering, Julian, *The Chatham Directory of Inshore Craft: Traditional Working Vessels of the British Isles* (Chatham: London, 1997)

Griffiths, Maurice, *Sixty years a Yacht Designer* (Conway Maritime Press: London, 1988)

Harris, Keith, *Azook: The Story and History of the Pilot Gigs of Cornwall and the Isles of Scilly 1666-1993* (Dyllansow Truran: Redruth, 1994)

Hazell, Martin, *Sailing Barges*, Third Edition (Shire Books: 2001)

Hempel, J.C., (ed.), *Your Ship And Its Maintenance*, Second Edition (Copenhagen, 1965)

Facing page: This print shows Captain Cook's ship, Endeavour, badly damaged after running aground on the Great Barrier Reef in June 1770. The ship has been 'careened' or leant over so the damage can be inspected and repaired.

Kearon, John, *'Emily Barratt' Survey & Condition Report; Survey Analysis; Proposals for the Display of Wooden Boats at Barrow Dock Museum* (National Museums and Galleries on Merseyside, 1996)

Kearon, John, *Fricka: The Conservation and Restoration of a Victorian Yacht* (typescript: 2004)

Kearon, John, *The Ladies Gig: The Conservation of a Wooden Victorian Pulling Gig.* (Personal archive, unpublished)

Kemp, Peter, *The History of Ships* (Orbis Books: London, 1978)

Kemp, Peter, (ed.), *The Oxford Companion to Ships and the Sea* (Oxford University Press: Oxford, 1988)

Kentley, Eric, Stephens, Simon & Heighton, Martyn, *Understanding Historic Vessels Volume 1: Recording Historic Vessel* (National Historic Ships: London, 2007)

Kentley, Eric, Stephens, Simon & Heighton, Martyn, *Understanding Historic Vessels Volume 2: Deconstructing Historic Vessels* (National Historic Ships: London, 2007)

Kerr, James Semple, *The Conservation Plan* (National Trust: New South Wales, 1996)

King, Andy, Lavery, Brian, Tanner, Matthew and Young, Chris (eds.), *A Manual of Maritime Curatorship* (Maritime Curators Group: 2002)

Kittridge, Alan, *Cornwall's Maritime Heritage: with special places to visit* (Twelveheads Press: Truro, 2003)

Knight, RJB, *A Guide to the Manuscripts in the National Maritime Museum* (Mansell: London, 1980)

Knowles, John, *An Inquiry into the methods which have been taken to preserve the British Navy* (London, 1821)

Knox-Johnston, Robin, *The Twilight of Sail* (Putnam: New York, 1979)

Larn, Richard and Bridget, *Charlestown*, Second Edition (Tor Mark: Redruth, 2006)

Lenton, W. Stewart, *The Fishing Boats & Ports of Cornwall: An Alternative Way to Explore Cornwall* (Channel View Publishing: Plymouth, 2006)

Lewis, John, *Vintage Boats* (David & Charles: Newton Abbot, 1975)

Light, Tim, Brightley, Lucy and Budd, Tony, *King Harry's Cornwall: Guide Book* (2007)

Lipke, Paul, Spectre, Peter and Fuller, Benjamin, (eds.), *Boats: A Manual for Their Documentation* (Museum Small Craft Association, American Association for State and Local History: Tennessee, 1993)

Littlewood, Kevin and Butler, Beverley, *Of Ships and Stars: Maritime Heritage and the Foundings of the National Maritime Museum* (The Athlone Press: London, 1998)

Lunn, Iver, *Antifouling: A brief introduction to the origins and development of the marine antifouling industry* (BCA Publications: Oxon, 1974)

Lyon, David, *The Sailing Navy List: All the Ships of the Royal Navy – Built, Purchased and Captured – 1688-1860* (Conway: London, 2001)

MacGregor, David R., *Schooners in Four Centuries* (Argus Books Ltd: Herts, 1982)

MacGregor, David R., *Fast Sailing Ships: Their Design and Construction, 1775-1875* (Conway: London, 1988)

Mathias, Peter, and Pearsall, A.W.H., (eds.), *Shipping: A Survey of Historical Records* (David & Charles: Newton Abbot, 1971)

McKee, Eric, *Working Boats of Britain: Their Shape and Purpose* (Conway Maritime Press: London, 1983)

Newby, Eric, *Learning the Ropes: an apprentice in the last of the windjammers* (John Murray: London, 1999)

Paasch, H., *From Keel to Truck: A Marine Dictionary* (Antwerp, 1885)

Paton, John, Commander RN, and Kentley, Dr Eric, *Shipping Forecast Part One: Towards a policy for the United Kingdom's historic fleet. Interim Report 1: A review of the National Historic Ships Committee's Core Collection* (2003)

Plenderleith, H.J., The *Conservation of Antiquities and Works of Art: Treatment, Repair, and Restoration* (OUP, 1969)

Ponsford, Clive N., *Shipbuilding on the Exe: The Memoranda Book of Daniel Bishop Davy (1799-1874) of Topsham, Devon.* (Devon and Cornwall Record Society, Vol.31, 1988)

Rasmussen, Tom, *Flytende kulturminner. En innføring i fartøyvern* (Direktoratet for kulturminnevern: Oslo, 1998)

Ritchie L.A., (ed.), *The Shipbuilding Industry: A Guide to Historical Records* (Manchester University Press: Manchester, 1992)

Sagar-Fenton, Michael, *The Rosebud and the Newlyn Clearances* (Truran: Truro, 2003)

Scarlett, John, *Wooden Boats: Restoration & Maintenance Manual* (David & Charles: Newton Abbot, 1987)

Scott, C. J. de C. Lieutenant Commander, Royal Navy (ed.), *The Mariner's Handbook*, Third Edition (Hydrographer of the Navy, 1971)

Scott, Richard J., *The Story of the Kathleen & May.* Second Edition (The Maritime Trust: 1987)

Slocum, Capt. Joshua, *Sailing Alone Around The World* (Adlard Coles Nautical: London, 2006)

Smith, Hervey Garrett, *Boat Carpentry*, Second Edition (Van Nostrand Reinhold: USA, 1965)

Stammers, Michael, *End of Voyages: The Afterlife of a Ship* (Tempus: Glous, 2004)

Stammers, Michael and Kearon, John, *The Jhelum: A Victorian Merchant Ship* (Sutton Publishing: Bath, 1992)

Standards in the Museum Care of Larger and Working Objects: Social and Industrial History Collections No 4 (Museums & Galleries Commission: 1994)

Steffy, J. Richard, *Wooden Ship Building and the Interpretation of Shipwrecks* (Texas UP, 2006)

Stewart, W. Roderick, *Welcome Abroad: The Frigate Unicorn* (Unicorn Preservation Society: Dundee, 1982)

Tanner, Matthew, *The Ship and Boat Collection of Merseyside Maritime Museum: An Illustrated Catalogue* (Merseyside Maritime Museum, 1995)

The Dog Watch: Restoration of Ships in Australia, No. 48. (Shiplovers' Society of Victoria, Australia, 1991)

The Secretary of the Interior's *Standards for Historic Vessel Preservation Projects with Guidelines for Applying the Standards* (National Maritime Initiative: USA, 1990)

The Scottish Fisheries Museum, Anstruther, Guidebook (n.d.)

Walker, Meredith and Marquis-Kyle, Peter, *The Illustrated Burra Charter: Good Practice for Heritage Places* '(Australia ICOMOS Inc: Burwood, 2004)

Ward-Jackson, C. H., *Ships and Shipbuilders of a West Country Seaport: Fowey 1786-1939* (Twelveheads: Truro, 1986)

Warren, Nigel, *Metal Corrosion in Boats: The prevention of metal corrosion in hulls, engines, rigging and fittings*, Second Edition (Adlard Coles Nautical: London, 1998)

Watson, Jonathan, *Janet: The Restoration of a Victorian Yacht* (David & Charles: Newton Abbot, 1986)

Welch, George S., *The Ship Painter's Handbook* (Glasgow, 1927)

Williams, Alan and Clark, Catherine, *A River Severn Trow at Lydney, Gloucestershire: An Archaeological and Naval Architectural Investigation* for English Heritage. Ironbridge Archaeological Series No 27 (March 1992)

Wilson, David, *Falmouth Haven: The Maritime History of a Great West Country Port* (Tempus: Glous, 2007)

Winkworth, Kylie and Australian Heritage Projects, *Review of existing criteria for assessing significance relevant to movable heritage collections and objects.* Department of Communications and the Arts (October 1998)

....

ARTICLES

Anderson, Richard K., 'Lifting Lines from the Schooner *Wawona*', The Journal of the Association for Preservation Technology, Vol.IX, No.1 (1987) pp.80-88.

Barlow, Alec, 'The Fastenings Used in the Construction and Subsequent Restoration of HMS *Victory*', *The Mariner's Mirror*, Vol.85, No.1 (February 1999), pp.79-82

Barnard, Matt, 'Is Britain's maritime heritage sinking?', *Museums Journal*, Vol.100, No.10 (October 2000), pp.20-23

Brouwer, Norman, 'The Role of Historical Research in Documenting Historic Vessels', *The Journal of the Association for Preservation Technology*, Vol.IX, No.1 (1987) pp.40-43

Birkholz, Don, 'The Role of Marine Surveys in Maritime Preservation', *The Journal of the Association for Preservation Technology*, Vol.IX, No.1 (1987) pp.44-45

'Conclusion: Towards a National Policy for Maritime Preservation', *The Journal of the Association for Preservation Technology*, Vol.IX, No.1 (1987) pp.78-79

Darr, Bob, 'Maritime Preservation Training Programs', *The Journal of the Association for Preservation Technology*, Vol.IX, No.1 (1987) pp.76-77

Delgado, James P., 'The National Register of Historic Places and Maritime Preservation', *The Journal of the Association for Preservation Technology*, Vol.IX, No.1 (1987) pp.34-39.

Farrar, Austin P., 'Recording a Craft's Lines', *The Mariner's Mirror*, Vol.82, No.2 (May 1996), pp.216-222

Goodwin, Peter, 'The Fore Topsail of HMS Victory', *The Mariner's Mirror*, Vol.83, No.1 (February 1997), pp.90-91

Greenwood, Steve, 'Entrance fees simply aren't a major factor', *Museums Journal*, Vol.100, No.10 (October 2000), pp.28-29

Hewson, Dana, 'Suggested Standards for the Maintenance of Historic Vessels', *The Journal of the Association for Preservation Technology*, Vol.IX, No.1 (1987) pp.72-75

Kearon, John, 'The NMGM approach to Ship and Boat Conservation' in Dollery, D. and J. Henderson, *Industrial Collections: Care and Conservation*. Council for the Museums in Wales/ United Kingdom Institute for Conservation (1997) pp.91-99

Kortum, Karl, 'Why Do We Save Ships?', *The Journal of the Association for Preservation Technology*, Vol.IX, No.1 (1987) pp.30-33.

Maounis, John, 'Interpreting Historic Vessels', *The Journal of the Association for Preservation Technology*, Vol.IX, No.1 (1987) pp.62-65

McGrath, H. Thomas, James P. Delgado and Don Birkholz, 'Historic Structure Report: WAPAMA', *The Journal of the Association for Preservation Technology*, Vol.IX, No.1 (1987) pp.4-9

McKee, Eric, 'Traditional British Boatbuilding Methods', *The Mariner's Mirror*, Vol.62 (1976) pp.3-14

Morss, Strafford, 'Preserving the Warships of World War II, Battleship Cove as a Case History', *The Journal of the Association for Preservation Technology*, Vol.IX, No.1 (1987) pp.56-59.

Murphy, Larry, 'Preservation at Pearl Harbour', *The Journal of the Association for Preservation Technology*, Vol.IX, No.1 (1987) pp.10-15

Nash, Michael A., 'The Fore Topsail of HMS *Victory*', *The Mariner's Mirror*, Vol.83, No.3 (August 1997), pp.347-348

Neill, Peter, 'Developing a National Cultural Policy for Maritime Preservation', *The Journal of the Association for Preservation Technology*, Vol.IX, No.1 (1987) pp.24-29.

Rybka, Walter, 'Preserving Historic Vessels: A Long View of History' and 'Suggested Standards for Replica and Reproduction Vessels', *The Journal of the Association for Preservation Technology*, Vol.IX, No.1 (1987) pp.46-52 and pp.66-71

Steele, Peter, 'Artefacts Within Artefacts Collections and Historic Vessels', *The Journal of the Association for Preservation Technology*, Vol.IX, No.1 (1987) pp.60-61

Thomson, Peter, 'Working a Thames Sailing Barge circa 1950', *The Mariner's Mirror*, Vol.81, No.4 (November 1995), pp.457-462

Waite, Simon, '*Cutty Sark*: Restoration of the Mizzen Lower Mast', *The Mariner's Mirror*, Vol.86, No.2 (May 2000), pp.206-212

Walker, David A., 'The Application of Preservation Technology to Historic Ships', *The Journal of the Association for Preservation Technology*, Vol.IX, No.1 (1987) pp.53-55.

Wall, Glennie Murray, 'The National Maritime Initiative', *The Journal of the Association for Preservation Technology*, Vol.IX, No.1 (1987) pp.2-3

Weaver, Martin, 'Fighting Rust', *The Journal of the Association for Preservation Technology*, Vol.IX, No.1 (1987) pp.16-18

....

CONFERENCE/ MEETING PAPERS

Technical Aspects of Maintaining, Repairing & Preserving Historically Significant Ships. Conference hosted by United States Department of the Interior, held at Naval Historical Center Detachment, Boston, 12, 13, 14 September 1994.

Agenda & Programme

Anon, USS *Constitution*. 'Dimensions and Sizes of Materials for Building a Frigate of Forty-Four Guns', from Joshua Humphreys' Letter Book, 1793-1787, pp.99-112'.

Baker, Andrew J., 'Corrosion of Metal Fasteners in Wood'.

Booth, Russell, 'Developing and Implementing a Long-Term Preservation Plan. Example: USS *Pampanito* (SS-383)'.

Booth, Russell, 'Problem Areas on World War II Submarines. Example: USS *Pampanito* (SS-383)'.

Kearon, John, 'Caring for Ships in a Museum Environment'.

Kearon, John, 'Preserving the Maritime Heritage', *Proceedings of the 2nd International Symposium of the Conservation and Restoration of Cultural Property* (1998) pp.124-133, Tokyo National Research Institute of Cultural Property

Lynaugh, Kevin, 'Discussion of the Loads, Structure, and Monitoring of Them in Order to Reduce the Hogging of the USS *Constitution*'.

Morgan, T. Fraser, 'HMS *Warrior* 1860: Maintenance and Docking Issues'.

Morss, Strafford, 'Standards for Steel Ships'.

Prescott, Robert G.W., 'Abstract – The Frigate *Unicorn*'.

Robinson, John, 'Look to the Privateers: Partnership in the Care of Historic Boats'.

Smith, David and Bridgewater, Tony. 'The Restoration of HMS *Trincomalee*'.

Steele, Peter, 'To Rehabilitate a Warship. USS *Cassin Young*'.

Tanner, Matthew, 'Ship and Boat Preservation – A place for original fabric'.

Wenzel, John, 'HMS *Belfast* – Hull Condition Evaluation'.

McMurray, Campbell, 'The Museological Case for the Preservation of M33'. Paper originally presented to the M33 (HMS *Minerva*) Steering Committee, 11 January 1995. Typescript.

Tanner, Matthew, *Note on Conservation Planning for Ships*. Big Ships Forum, 23 July 1998. Typescript.

Robinson, John, Report, Agenda Item 5c, Curatorial. Eighty-Fourth Meeting of the Trustees of the Royal Naval Museum, 8 July 2005. Typescript.

White, Colin, '*The Archaeology of Ships of War': Too many preserved ships threaten the heritage*. National Maritime Museum, Oxford University MARE, World Ship Trust, Nautical Archaeology Society, 31 October - 1 November 1992. Typescript.

Aircraft to Artefact. Proceedings of a conference on Aviation Historic Preservation, Royal Air Force Museum, Hendon, 1 -2 September 1990. Typescript.

....

Index

F = Foreword
I = Image Caption

Air-conditioned – 120 (l)

Allied Forces – 76 (l)

Apprenticeship – 149

Archaeologist – 58

Archive(s) – 6, 16, 24, 63, 66, 67, 68, 69, 125, 177

Archivist(s) – 69

Art Deco – 175

Barcelona Charter – 27

Bartlett Library – 69

Battle of Trafalgar – 22 (l), 75, 75 (l), 132 (l), 174 (l), 175

Bilge(s) – 67 (l), 184, 185, 188, 193, 195

Boatbuilding – 57 (l)

Bolshevik Revolution – 83

British – 24, 47, 67, 68, 76 (l), 170

British Library – 68

Budget(s) – 39, 91

Buoyancy – 156, 177

Business plan – 31, 78, 101

Caird Library – 67

Charitable organisations – 101

Classic Boat – 27, 69

Cleaning cycle – 184

Coating(s) – 58, 92, 116, 119, 120, 141, 142, 146, 185, 188

Commercial – 6, 7 (l), 15, 23, 68, 93, 146, 149, 158, 175

Condition survey – 36, 39, 41, 102, 103

Conservation management plan – 30-31, 39, 80, 100, 101, 198

Conservator(s) – 39, 48, 58, 192, 116, 102, 122, 125

Consultant – 100

Cornish – 170

Corrosion – 47, 120, 122, 122 (l), 125, 184, 185, 188

COUNTRIES

Australia / Australian(s) – 27, 76, 170 (l), 172

Denmark – 28, 173 (l)

Europe – 27, 28, 30, 83

France – 28

Ireland – 27, 115 (l), 119, 125

Netherlands – 28

Norway – 28, 125, 170

Poland – 170

USA – 28

Covers – 46 (l), 47, 48, 68, 91, 185, 186, 191

Curator(s) – 29, 91, 119, 197

Deconstructing – 10, 102

Deconstruction – F, 103, 168

Dehumidification – 47, 122 (l)

Disabled access – 156

Drawing(s) – 24, 57, 58, 60, 61 (l), 63, 65, 66, 68, 79 (l), 120, 130, 146, 168, 172, 173

Dry dock – 24, 47, 91, 92, 94, 101 (l), 102, 122 (l), 149, 183

Dutch – 132

Easter Rising – 125

Edwardian – 175

Engineer(s) – 39, 116, 122, 125, 168 (l)

Engineering – 66, 76

Engine(s) – 48, 66, 67, 135, 144, 145, 149, 154, 158 (l), 166, 168 (l), 170, 172, 173, 174, 175 (l), 184, 188, 193

English – 76, 169

Environment(s) – 6, 9, 23, 27, 40, 46, 48, 76, 88, 88 (l), 91, 94, 116, 118, 119, 120, 122 (l), 123, 125, 145, 182, 184, 186, 189, 199, 200
Environmental – 91, 116, 120

Fastening(s) – 9, 58, 60, 120, 125, 141, 142, 168

Ferrous – 9, 47, 119, 120

First aid – 47, 48, 50 (l), 65

Fuel – 188

Funding – 13, 27, 28, 29, 29 (l), 30, 46, 47 (l), 74, 100, 144, 167, 177

Graffiti – 23, 119

Grant(s) – F, 27, 28, 29, 30, 31, 46, 80, 92, 100, 100 (l), 101, 144, 149, 168 (l)

Grant aid – F, 27, 28, 29, 30, 80, 92, 100 (l), 101, 168 (l)

GRP – 185

Guildhall Library – 68

Hardwood(s) – 169, 170 (l)

Herring – 26 (l), 118, 158

Humidity – 47, 183, 185

Hulks – 47

Hydraulic – 156

Illustrated Burra Charter – 27

IMO regulations – 94

Infestation – 120, 189

Insurance – 40, 41, 154

Irish – 125, 132

Kirk Collection – 69

Lloyd's List – 67

Lloyd's Register of Shipping – 67, 68, 69

Lloyd's Register of Yachts – 69

Log books – 149

Maintenance plan – 19, 31, 184, 185 (l), 186, 188

Maritime Life & Traditions – 69 (l)

Mashford Floats – 156

Mercantile Navy List – 67

Milton – 192

Model(s) – 25 (l), 67 (l), 69, 74, 118, 154, 168 (l), 173

Monument(s) – 24, 28, 29

Mouldings – 119

Museum (s) – F, 6, 7, 9 (l), 19, 23, 24, 25, 26 (l), 27, 28, 29, 29 (l), 30, 40, 47 (l), 48, 58, 66 (l), 67, 68, 69, 88 (l), 91, 100, 101, 109, 115, 115 (l), 116, 118, 118 (l), 119, 120, 120 (l), 122, 125, 130 (l), 132, 132 (l), 141, 141 (l), 142 (l), 145, 145 (l), 170, 170 (l), 172, 182, 197, 201

Naval architect – 58, 94, 146

Navy List – 68

Object file – 120

Oceanographic – 79

Operation Dynamo – 76

Operational manual – 195

Oral history – 56, 58, 60, 63, 177

ORGANISATIONS

Advisory Committee on National Historic Ships (ACNHS) – F, 27

Australian National Maritime Museum – 170 (l), 172

BBC – 57

British Rail – 170

Cambria Trust – 149

Cardiff University – 122, 125

City College Plymouth – 6 (l)

Coastal Craft Committee – 24

Cutty Sark Society – 25

Department of Culture, Media and Sport (DCMS) – F, 28

Dundee Heritage Trust – 79 (l)

Dunkirk Little Ships – 76

English Heritage (EH) – 27, 28, 64

Environment and Heritage Service – 27

European Maritime Heritage – 27

Falmouth Marine School – 118

French Navy – 119

Heritage Lottery fund (HLF) – 27, 30, 46, 100 (l), 149, 167

Historic Scotland – 27

Imperial War Museum – 25, 29, 29 (l)

International Sailing Craft Association – 24

Ironbridge Gorge Museum – 141 (l)

Lakeland Arts Trust – 135

Local Planning Authority – 80

Lyme Regis Boat Building Academy – 177

Maritime Trust – 25, 27

MCA – 102, 144, 146, 154, 156, 172, 186, 195, 200

Merseyside Maritime Museum – 25, 29, 48, 68, 119, 130 (l), 132, 142 (l), 170

Mystic Seaport Museum – 28

National Antarctic Expedition – 79

National Archive of Historic Vessels (NAHV) – 28

National Heritage Memorial Fund – 30, 135

National Historic Fleet (NHF) – F, 10, 28, 29, 39 (l), 101 (l), 199

National Maritime Museum (NMM) – 9 (l), 23, 24, 25, 66 (l), 67, 68, 69, 132 (l), 170 (l)

National Maritime Museum Cornwall (NMMC) – F, 28, 69, 88 (l), 118, 118 (l), 145, 145 (l)

National Museum of Ireland – 115 (l), 119, 125

National Museums Liverpool – 29, 119

National Register of Historic Vessels (NRHV) – F, 10, 27, 38, 199

National Small Boat Register (NSBR) – F, 10, 28

National Waterways Museum – 47 (l)

Navy – 30 (l), 47, 58 (l), 68, 69, 83, 94 (l), 119, 132, 154

Navy Board – 68, 69

Norfolk Wherry Trust – 25

Paddle Steamer Preservation Society – 154 (l)

Portsmouth University – 122

Queen Elizabeth Trust – 177

RNLI – 141 (l), 161

Royal Cruising Club (RCC) – 69

Royal Yachting Association (RYA) – 69

Royal Yacht Squadron (RYS) – 69

Science Museum – 23, 24

Scottish Fisheries Museum – 26 (l), 170, 182

Society for Nautical Research (SNR) – F, 24

Textile Conservation Centre – 75 (l)

Thames Sailing Barge Club – 24

The King's Regiment – 47

The National Archives – 69

Unicorn Preservation Society – 58 (l)

University of Glasgow – 67

University of Liverpool – 68

Vikingeskibsmuseet – 174

Viking Ship Museum – 170

Welsh Assembly CADW – 27

Passenger(s) – standfirst, F, 76, 94, 135, 154, 172, 182 (I), 186, 199

Passive conservation – 118

PEOPLE

ANZAC – 83

Archer, Colin – 125

Beken (of Cowes) – 69

Brunel, Isambard Kingdom – 74, 145

Cabot, John – 175, 175 (I)

Carr, Frank – 24, 25

Childers, Erskine – 7 (I), 125

Churchill, Sir Winston – 83

Clark, Kate – 27

Cook (Captain) – 170 (I), 172

Crossfields of Arneside – 142

Cunliffe, Ros – 191

Cunliffe, Tom – 191

Drake, Francis – 24

Edinburgh (Duke of) – 25

Elizabeth I (Queen) – 24

Elizabeth II (Queen) – 182 (I)

Everard, William – 149

Everett, John – 186 (I)

Fife, William – 145

Fisher, Admiral Sir Jacky – 83

Forrest & Son – 135

Frith, Francis – 69

George V (King) – 56 (I)

Giles, Laurent – 93

Goldsack, Tim – 149

Gollop, Roy – 177

Heyerdahl, Thor – 174

Kearon, John – 119, 125

Kerr, James Semple – 74

Lapenotiere (Lieutenant) – 174 (I)

Lillicrap, Charles – 83

Lipton, Sir Thomas – 28

Mann, Robert – 145 (I)

McGarva, Gail – 176-177

Moody, A. H. – 93

Nelson – 24

Pattinson, George – 135

Payne, William – 183 (I)

Roberts, Bob – 149

Severin, Tim – 174

Sisson & Co – 135

Slocum, Joshua – 141

Scott of the Antarctic – 79

Tennyson d'Eyncourt, Sir Eustace – 83

Trollope – 76

Peppercorn A1 Pacific Class – 170

Photographs – 38 (I), 57, 63, 65, 68, 69, 130, 168, 173, 177

PLACE NAMES

Appledore – 101 (I), 118

Atlantic – 23, 29 (I), 80 (I)

Bantry Bay – 119

Bermondsey – 63 (I)

Bjorkedalan – 170

Blists Hill – 141

Bristol – 74 (I), 141 (I), 175, 191

Bristol Channel – 141

Brittany – 93

Cape Horn – 182

Channel (the) – 30, 141 (I), 183

Chatham – 24, 30 (I), 58, 58 (I), 91 (I), 94 (I), 154 (I), 161

Chesil Beach – 177

Chester – 170

Clovelly – 118, 118 (I)

Colindale – 68

Connecticut – 28

Continent (the) – 149

Conway – 48 (I), 66 (I), 68 (I)

Cowes – 56 (I), 69

Cumbria – 142

Deptford – 24

Dorset – 177

Dublin – 115 (I), 173 (I), 174

Dundee – 58 (I), 79 (I)

Dunkirk – 76, 76 (I)

East India Dock – 64 (I)

Edinburgh – 25, 68, 92

Falklands (the) – 46 (I), 47, 57

Falmouth – 101 (I), 118, 145

Faversham – 149

Flamborough – 161

Gallipoli – 83

Gladstone Graving Dock – 80 (I)

Glasgow - 67, 68, 145 (I)

Gloucester – 135

Gota Canal – 168 (I)

Hull – 68

Irish Sea – 132

Isles of Scilly – 166 (I)

Isle of Wight – 56 (I)

Kent – 149

Leith – 92

Liverpool – 29, 46 (I), 47, 68, 80 (I), 119

Melbourne – 76

Mersey (Merseyside) – 25, 29, 48, 68, 119, 130 (I), 132, 142 (I), 170

Millwall – 63 (I)

Newcastle – 68

Newfoundland – 175

Norfolk – 125, 184 (I)

Normandy – 76 (I)

North Devon – 101 (I)

North Russia – 83

Oslo – 170

Oxford – 24

Plymouth – 6

Portsmouth – 9 (I), 24, 122

Port Stanley – 47

Richmond Dock – 101 (I)

River Dee – 170

River Medina – 100 (I)

Rochefort – 132 (I)

Roskilde – 28, 174

Rotherhithe – 68 (I)

Sandar – 170

Scotland – 67, 167 (I)

Seaham – 102 (I), 161

Sittingbourne – 149

Skuldelev – 174

Solent – 25, 69

Somerset – 149

Southampton – 101 (I)

Southwold – 184 (I)

St Katharine's Dock – 27

Stockholm – 115, 191

St. Petersburg – 175

Suffolk – 184 (I)

Texas – 186 (I)

Tilbury – 183

Tooley Street – 67

Trafalgar – 22 (I) 24, 75, 75 (I), 132 (I), 174 (I), 175

Western Isles – 167 (I)

Windermere – 135

Wivenhoe – 135

Plan(s) – 23, 24, 38 (I), 60, 66 (I), 68, 166 (I), 168, 170 (I), 171, 172, 173

Poly-ethylene glycol – 116, 120 (I)

Practical Boat Owner – 69

Preventive conservation – 118

Private owner (s) – 7, 7 (I), 23, 27, 28, 30, 38, 40, 46, 60, 63, 69, 80, 91, 93, 94, 100, 101, 154, 191, 201

Project diary – 125

Project plan – 135

Public – 6, 23, 25, 27, 28, 29, 30, 75, 83, 88, 92, 93, 94, 94 (I), 100, 101, 102, 109, 115, 116, 120 (I), 145, 156 (I), 184 (I), 186, 199

Recording – F, 10, 20, 24, 36, 47, 102, 103, 120, 146, 195, 198

Record office(s) – 68

Rot – 9, 47, 102, 116, 144, 184, 185, 186, 189, 120

Royal Family - 92

Rust – 47, 102, 116, 120, 144, 184, 185, 186

Scandinavian – 170

Scientists – 116

Second World War – 141 (I), 154 (I)

Shipbuilding – 67, 68

Shipwrights – 23, 48, 58, 102, 116, 122, 125, 146, 149

Skill(s) – F, 9, 10, 21, 23, 24, 28, 29, 38, 50, 57, 58, 91, 93, 101, 116, 122, 132, 142, 144, 159

SOLAS – 94

Sponsors – 168 (I)

Spot-listing – 29

Stability – 51, 120, 156

Staff – 48, 100, 135, 154

Statement of significance – 19, 74, 80, 83, 100

Stockholm tar – 191

Student(s) – 6 (I), 118

Sulphuric acid – 116

Survey Report(s) – 67, 195

Swedish – 120 (I), 170

Tarpaulin(s) – 47 (I)

Thesis – 58

The Times – 68

The Yachtsman – 69

Timber – 58, 116, 122, 142, 144 (I), 148, 169, 170 (I)

Tornado – 170

Trustee(s) – F, 31, 40, 91, 100

Varnol – 191

Ventilation – 46, 47, 48, 51, 120, 158, 184, 185

VESSEL NAMES

Agnes – 166 (l)

Aguila Wren – 141 (l)

Alaska – 182 (l)

Alfred Corry – 184 (l)

Aquitania – 80 (l)

Asgard – 7 (l), 115 (l), 124, 125

Bantry Boat – 116 (l), 119

Box Boat – 47 (l)

Birkdale – 186 (l)

Brendon – 174

Britannia – 56 (l)

Cambria – 148-149

Cutty Sark – 25, 64 (l)

Daystar – 142 (l)

De Wadden – 25, 29, 130 (l), 132

Droleen II – 93

Duguay-Trouin – 132 (l)

Edith May – 46

Edmund Gardner – 25, 29

Endeavour – 170 (l), 172

Ferriby Boats – 24

Framlington Court – 67 (l)

Fricka – 145, 145 (l)

Gaia – 170

George Elmy – 102 (l)

Gokstad Ship – 170

Golden Hinde – 24

Greek Trireme – 174

Helen II – 48 (l), 49 (l)

Helen Smitton – 158 (l)

HM Frigate *Unicorn* – 58, 58 (l)

HM Schooner *Pickle* – 174 (l), 175

HMS *Belfast* – 25, 29, 29 (l), 182

HMS *Cavalier* – 154 (l), 156

HMS *Gannet* – 94 (l), 100 (l)

HMS *Trincomalee* – 56

HMS *Victory* – F, 22 (l), 24, 75, 75 (l), 119, 156, 170

HMS *Warrior* – 8 (l), 9 (l), 23, 66 (l), 92, 94

HMY *Britannia* – 92, 94

Holland I – 122

Ilyrica – 56 (l)

Implacable – 132 (l)

Jane – 141

J G Graves of Sheffield – 161

Jhelum – 46 (l), 47, 48, 61 (l)

Kon Tiki – 174

Ladies gig – 40 (l)

Little Mary – 118, 118 (l)

Lizzie May – 167 (l)

M33 – 82, 83, 122

Mary Rose – 25, 88, 91, 116

Matthew – 175, 175 (l)

Medusa – 10 (l)

Miss Britain – 9 (l)

Nordevall – 168 (l), 169 (l), 170

Ocelot – 30

Olympias – 174

Otto – 134 (l), 135

ps *Ryde* – 98-99 (l), 100 (l)

ps *Waverley* – 152–153 (l), 1544 (l), 156

Ra II – 174

Reaper – 26 (l), 156 (l), 158 182, 185 (l)

RRS *Discovery* – 79, 79 (l)

Sea Stallion – 173, 173 (l), 174

Spray – 141, 142

Spry – 141

SS *Aguila* – 141

ss *Great Britain* – 57, 66, 72-73 (l), 74 (l), 76, 115 (l), 122, 145, 156, 157 (l)

SS *Robin* – 34-35 (l), 36 (l), 39 (l), 106, 107 (l)

SS *Shieldhall* – 101 (l)

Temeraire – 68 (l)

Terpsichore – 56 (l)

Vasa – 88, 115, 116, 120 (l), 121 (l)

Vera – 177

Westernman – 190-193 (l)

Will & Fanny Kirby – 160 (l), 161

VESSEL TYPES

Auxiliary schooner – 130 (l), 132

Barge(s) – 24, 25, 26 (l), 63 (l), 116 (l), 119, 149, 182 (l)

Barque – 186 (l)

Canoe(s) – 24

Cargo vessel – 23, 67 (l), 141 (l), 149, 170 (l)

Carrack – 175

Coracle(s) – 24, 25 (l)

Cutter – 25, 29, 166 (l), 167 (l), 170, 191

Dredger(s) – 23, 132, 198

Ferries – 175

Fifie – 26 (l), 158, 182, 185 (l)

Fishing punt – 23

Freighter(s) – 23

Fully-rigged ship – 170

Hospital ship – 92

Houseboat – 23

Ironclad – 66 (l)

Lerret – 170, 176 (l), 177

Lifeboat(s) – 67, 67 (l), 91 (l), 102 (l), 104 (l), 141 (l), 156, 158, 161, 184 (l)

Liner – 80 (l)

Longship – 174

Merchant ship – 46 (l), 47, 60, 61 (l), 67, 69, 130 (l)

Morecambe Bay Prawner – 48, 142

Motor boat(s) – 23

Naval monitor – 83

Nobby – 142

Oakley class – 161

Paddle steamer – Standfirst, 100 (l), 154 (l), 156, 168 (l)

Passenger vessel – F, 182

Picarooner – 118, 118 (l)

Pilot cutter(s) – 25, 29, 166 (l), 167 (l), 191

Raft(s) – 24

Rowing boat – 91

Salmon boat – 170

Sand dredger – 132

Severn trow – 141

Skiffs – 170

Steam yacht – 135

Storage hulk – 23

Thames half-rater – 142

Training ship – 23

Warship(s) – F, 6, 23, 25, 68, 83, 120 (l)

Watson lifeboat – 158 (l)

Wherries – 25

Yacht(s) – 7 (l), 23, (25), 28, 38, 56, 59, 69, 93, 125, 135, 145, 145 (l)

UK Disability Discrimination Act – 156

Ultra-violet light UV – 91, 186

Vandalism – 46, 122

Victorian – 94 (l), 145

Viking – 28, 170, 174

Visitor numbers – 27, 100

Volunteer(s) – 6, 26 (l), 31, 47, 80, 100, 101, 173 (l), 174, 182, 188

Waterlogged – 28, 88, 116

Wheelchair – 156, 157 (l)

Wooden Boat – 27

World War 1 – 83

Wreck(s) – 29, 58

Wrens – 141 (l)

Yachting Monthly – 24, 69

Yachting World - 69

213